T0354581

THE MIND

DON LITTON

authorHOUSE®

AuthorHouse™
1663 Liberty Drive
Bloomington, IN 47403
www.authorhouse.com
Phone: 1 (800) 839-8640

Published by AuthorHouse 08/15/2019

ISBN: 978-1-7283-2306-0 (sc)
ISBN: 978-1-7283-2305-3 (e)

Print information available on the last page.

This book is printed on acid-free paper.

The Holy Bible, King James Version, (KJV), New York: American Bible Society, 1999.

*The Holy Bible, New American Standard Bible, (NASB), La Habra, CA:
Foundation Publications, for the Lockman Foundation, 1971.*

*The Holy Bible, New International Version, (NIV), Grand
Rapids: Zondervan Publishing House, 1984.*

The Holy Bible, New Living Translation, (NLT), Tyndale House Foundation, 2015.

*The Holy Bible, Revised Standard Version Bible, (RSV), Division of Christian Education
of the National Council of the Churches of Christ in the United States of America, 1989*

CONTENTS

Romans 12:1-2 - *"Therefore, I urge you, brothers and sisters, in view of God's mercy, to offer your bodies as a living sacrifice, holy and pleasing to God—this is your true and proper worship. Do not conform to the pattern of this world, but be transformed by the renewing of your mind. Then you will be able to test and approve what God's will is—his good, pleasing and perfect will"* (**NIV**).

ACKNOWLEDGMENT

Writing a book was harder than I thought and more rewarding than I could have ever imagined. No one in life does anything worthwhile alone. So, in my case I have several special people to acknowledge. My wife, Janice, has kept me comforted and has for years put up with my crazy schedule, mainly my daytime and nighttime hours being in reverse order. Her love for Christ and me has allowed me great freedom to execute my calling. The members of Friendship Baptist Church in Fishville, La "endured my preaching and teaching" for 13 yrs, until January of 2018. They were a captive audience for my stories and not so humorous jokes; they would even groan when I began to tell them.

I would not have made it this far in my book had not my sister, Rita Litton Ellis, spent countless hours reading, correcting, and revising sentences and paragraphs of my manuscript. More importantly, I thank God for the journey, age 73, and to have KNOWN HIM for 58 years. Being a reborn Christian, the Lord has guided me with HIS eye and it has been an insane walk with HIM. Only a foolish man would say I know a lot about God because in my case the more I have learned about HIM, the less I realized I know.

Note: It's been said that a mind is a terrible thing to waste. And yet, that's exactly what most of us do intentionally and unintentionally. Dr Litton has mapped out how we can scripturally win the battle against Satan as he seeks to destroy our happiness and our witness by confusing our minds! It's a complex issue but the victory is ours if we follow the wisdom of the scriptures that Dr Litton has written/captured in this book. I'm honored and blessed to be a sponsor of this book!

Randy Wiggins

P.S. This man has been a State Farm Agent in Alexandria, LA for a number years and my friend and brother in Christ for over 50 years. Bless him and his family!

INTRODUCTION

God created the human mind as a combination of conscious and unconscious processes thoughts of the brain that direct our mental and physical behavior. Our thoughts influence our actions. It follows, then, that if we want to act like Christ, we must also think like Him. With the mind we exercise the power of reason, conceive ideas and use judgment. It stores our intellect, as distinguished from emotion or will.

The Importance of Your Mind

Many people do not realize the importance of having a sound mind until their own mind, or the mind of someone near to them, begins to show signs of instability in some way. Our mind is very important to us because it is our decision-making mechanism. If we lose an arm or a leg, we are, to some extent, restricted but can still make decisions and enjoy a reasonable quality of life. We can even lose some of our internal organs and yet continue to maintain a fair degree of independence. However, if we lose our mind, with it we lose also the ability to select our options and thus become dependent on others.

What say the Scriptures?

God in His Word, has a lot to say about the mind, which serves to further underline its crucial role. In **James**, we are told that a double-minded man is unstable in all his ways. Because he can't make up his mind, that man's whole life is one of instability.

James 1:8 - "A double minded man is unstable in all his ways" (**KJV**).

Matthew instructs us in:

Matthew 22:37 - "Jesus said unto him, Thou shalt love the Lord thy God with all thy heart, and with all thy soul, and with all thy mind" (**KJV**).

If we obey this command, how can it leave room for the mind to be infiltrated by Satan? We read in:

Romans 12.2 - "And be not conformed to this world: but be ye transformed by the renewing of your mind, that ye may prove what is that good, and acceptable, and perfect, will of God" (**KJV**).

Our lives are to be transformed and this transformation is brought about by renewing our minds.

CHAPTER 1

THE MIND

The **Mind** is a dangerous thing. It distorts situations, manipulates your emotions, and can trigger adrenaline in a millisecond. It can demand control, store/replay memories, and is unarguably one of the most powerful tools imaginable. A characteristic (1) feature of our **Mind** is that it keeps roaming and wandering; it operates in something like an automatic mode. Thoughts come and go all the time. If we attempt to suppress them, it is only possible with considerable efforts, and even then to a short time only. In most of our waking time, our Mind wanders either in the past or in the future, in our thoughts we deal with our experience of the past, offenses we suffered in the past, or with our future plans, goals and fears (Henriques, 2011).

Another characteristic (2) of our **Mind** is that it constantly evaluates things. It means that we do not simply live through our experiences, but we also categorize them as good or bad. We judge everything that happens to us and everybody we meet in our lives. This permanent categorization may easily lead to a distorted perception of the world, as we evaluate our new experiences in these categories. If we find an experience negative, we will tend to keep and reinforce that category for similar experiences in the future. Our perception will therefore be selective, and we will only accept the stimuli that reinforces our categorization, and we tend to ignore those that fall outside our usual categories (Henriques, 2011).

The third important characteristic (3) of the **Mind** is that it permanently produces stories. These stories often have a disastrous end. For instance, I suddenly try to remember whether I locked the door of my home or not. The Mind immediately fabricates a whole story around the idea: I did leave it open, a burglar came, my valuables have been stolen, and the police, instead of chasing the thief, will harass me with their questions. We often experience the ends and emotional consequences of these stories. Another type of stories deals with us, who are we, what are we like, what we should do or should have done. The entirety of these stories comprises our personal histories (Henriques, 2011).

Romans 8:6-8 - "For the mind set on the flesh is death, but the mind set on the Spirit is life and peace, because the mind set on the flesh is hostile toward God; for it does not subject itself to the law of God, for it is not even able *to do so*, and those who are in the flesh cannot please God" (**NASB**).

The mind of sinful man is death; the sinful mind is hostile to God. It does not submit to God's law, nor can it do so. Those controlled by the sinful nature cannot please God.

Titus 1:15 - "To the pure, all things are pure, but to those who are corrupted and do not believe, nothing is pure. In fact, both their minds and consciences are corrupted" (**NIV**).

Isaiah 55:7-8 - "Let the wicked forsake their ways and the unrighteous their thoughts. Let them turn to the LORD, and he will have mercy on them, and to our God, for he will freely pardon. "For my thoughts are not your thoughts, neither are your ways my ways," declares the LORD" (**NIV**).

As human beings, we prefer to do things our own way. As a result we can easily develop, either consciously or unconsciously, resentment toward God's authority over us.

Colossians 1:21 - "Once you were alienated from God and were enemies in your minds because of your evil behavior" (**NIV**).

This is especially true when His instruction forbids us to do as we wish. It then becomes easy for us to convert, usually unconsciously, our resentments, our underlying hostility toward what we may perceive as God's unnecessary interference in our affairs, into an active resistance to His commands. We simply begin to ignore some of His laws or reinterpret them to fit our own views. This is how our sinful nature, more commonly called *human nature*, works. These wrong attitudes begin in our minds.

We usually disguise resentful and disobedient attitudes to such an extent that we deceive ourselves into believing they do not exist. As Jeremiah observed:

Jeremiah 17:9 - "The heart is more deceitful than all else and is desperately sick; who can understand it" (**NASB**)?

We easily deceive ourselves into believing we are doing nothing wrong. That is why the Scriptures tells us in Proverbs:

Proverbs 14:12 - "There is a way that *seems right* to a man, but in the end it leads to death" (**NIV**).

We blind ourselves to the seriousness of our own sins. Everyone must face the problem of a sinful, deceitful mind. There are no exceptions. Resistance to God's instructions begins in our thoughts and attitudes. We have all sinned. We are all guilty.

- *Paul acknowledged his sinful nature?*

Romans 7:14-17 - "For we know that the law is spiritual; but I am of the flesh, sold into slavery under sin. I do not understand my own actions. For I do not do what I want, but I do the very thing I hate. Now if I do what I do not want, I agree that the law is good. But in fact it is no longer I that do it, but sin that dwells within me" (**RSV**).

Paul well understood his human nature, how deceitful it could be. As a young Jewish boy he had been taught to do what is right. In line with his early training, he was exceptionally sincere. Yet, when Christ opened his mind to see himself as he really was, he recognized he had deceived himself about his own righteousness. He could see he had sinned in many ways, both in action and attitude.

He concluded:

Romans 7:18-21 - "For I know that nothing good dwells within me, that is, within my flesh. I can will what is right, but I cannot do it. For I do not do the good I want, but the evil I do not want is what I do. Now if I do what I do not want, it is no longer I that do it, but sin that dwells within me. So I find it to be a law that when I want to do what is good, evil lies close at hand" (**RSV**).

Paul had not deliberately chosen to sin. Nevertheless, he could look back on his life and recognize that many things he had done were indeed sinful, though at the time he hadn't grasped that they were wrong and contrary to God's will. In describing his blindness to his own sinful actions and his weakness in resisting sin, he is describing every one of us (Henriques, 2011).

- *We must recognize our sins and deal with them?*

I John 1:8-10 - "If we say that we have no sin, we deceive ourselves, and the truth is not in us. If we confess our sins, He is faithful and just to forgive us our sins and to cleanse us from all unrighteousness. If we say that we have not sinned, we make Him a liar, and His word is not in us" (**NIV**).

James 1:13-15 - "When tempted, no one should say, "God is tempting me." For God cannot be tempted by evil, nor does he tempt anyone; but each person is tempted when they are dragged away by their own evil desire and enticed. Then, after desire has conceived, it gives birth to sin; and sin, when it is full-grown, gives birth to death" (**NIV**).

One of our great challenges is to recognize that our attitudes and actions often are not right in God's sight. We can convince ourselves that our own ways are fair and just. But to be truly converted to wholeheartedly turn to God, we must carefully and willingly examine our own motives. We must recognize we are all too susceptible to desires that channel our thinking down the pathways of sin.

Jesus explained that our priorities, what is most important to us, usually determines our actions. He cited the common problem of greed as an example:

Luke 16:13-15 - "No servant can serve two masters. Either he will hate the one and love the other, or he will be devoted to the one and despise the other. You cannot serve both God and Money.' The Pharisees, who loved money, heard all this and were sneering at Jesus. He said to them, 'You are the ones who justify yourselves in the eyes of men, but God knows your hearts. What is highly valued among men is detestable in God's sight'" (**NIV**).

What we cherish the most determines how we behave. When our values are flawed we look for ways to justify our views and behavior, deceiving ourselves.

James 1:22-24 - "Do not merely listen to the word, and so deceive yourselves. Do what it says. Anyone who listens to the word but does not do what it says is like someone who looks at his face in a mirror and, after looking at himself, goes away and immediately forgets what he looks like" (**NIV**).

- *What is a common self-deception?*

Mark 7:6-9 - "He replied, "Isaiah was right when he prophesied about you hypocrites; as it is written: "'These people honor me with their lips, but their hearts are far from me. They worship me in vain; their teachings are merely human rules.' You have let go of the commands of God and are holding on to human traditions." And he continued, "You have a fine way of setting aside the commands of God in order to observe your own traditions" (**NIV**).

Colossians 2:8 - "See to it that no one takes you captive through philosophy and empty deception, according to the tradition of men, according to the elementary principles of the world, rather than according to Christ" (**NASB**).

Traditions not solidly based on God's principles and laws often provide us with easy excuses to sin. Since almost everybody else practices them, we reason, how could they be wrong? But many times they are wrong. Jesus showed that common religious traditions, while outwardly appearing righteous, in reality can be disguising sin. For God said:

Matthew 15:4-6 - "Honor your father and mother' and 'Anyone who curses his father or mother must be put to death.' But you say that if a man says to his father or mother, 'Whatever help you might otherwise have received from me is a gift devoted to God,' he is not to 'honour his father' with it. Thus you nullify the word of God for the sake of your tradition" (**NIV**).

One of the reasons Christ died for us was to pay our penalty for following traditions contrary to the Scriptures. Conduct yourselves throughout the time of your stay here in fear, knowing that you were not redeemed with corruptible things, like silver or gold, from your aimless conduct received by tradition from your fathers, but with the precious blood of Christ, as of a lamb without blemish and without spot".

1 Peter 1:17-19 - "Since you call on a Father who judges each person's work impartially, live out your time as foreigners here in reverent fear. For you know that it was not with perishable things such as silver or gold that you were redeemed from the empty way of life handed down to you from your ancestors, but with the precious blood of Christ, a lamb without blemish or defect" (**NIV**).

It is important that we examine the traditions we follow to be sure they are not in conflict with the Word of God.

The sinful mind is hostile to God.

CHAPTER 2

GOD'S THINKING VS MAN'S THINKING

What are you thinking right now? Perhaps it's best that I don't know! Our minds are full of thoughts, our internal voice is often chatting away, meditating on the things that have gone, the things that are still to come, some of you might even be thinking about what I'm saying, but I know how easy it is for our mind to wander! But the real question is how are we thinking? Are we thinking like man or are we thinking like God? Of course, that's if it's even possible to think like the creator of the heavens and the earth! As always we will be using our Bibles to find the answers to our questions, because that's where God reveals his mind to us (Editor, 2019).

Isaiah 55:8-9 - "My thoughts are nothing like your thoughts," says the Lord. "And my ways are far beyond anything you could imagine. For just as the heavens are higher than the earth, so my ways are higher than your ways and my thoughts higher than your thoughts" (**NLT**).

I'd like you to keep this passage in our minds as we look at our topic. It's pretty clear that our thoughts are on a completely different plane to God's, there is this huge gulf between us and God, we naturally think differently to God, but why is that? How is our thinking different to God's thinking? Understanding this concept is one of the most important things we can do in our lives because it will naturally lead us in the right direction.

As often the case, the best place to start looking for answers is at the beginning. In **Genesis 3**, we read of Adam and Eve in the Garden of Eden, who were given one commandment by God which was to not eat the fruit of the tree of the knowledge of good and evil.

Genesis 3:1 - "The serpent was the shrewdest of all the wild animals the Lord God had made. One day he asked the woman, "Did God really say you must not eat the fruit from any of the trees in the garden" (**NLT**)?

Genesis 3:4 - "You won't die!" the serpent replied to the woman" (**NLT**).

This was a lie, a big lie, as God had said earlier they would die if they ate the fruit he had told them not to eat. God has told us that if we break his commandments then there will be severe consequences and we will die. So for breaking his commandment there was punishment for Adam and Eve, all of mankind, and the serpent, and here is where the struggle between good and evil begins. There is going to be this constant struggle between the nature of man and the nature of God, with man naturally prone to sin and God unable to tolerate sin you can see how this conflict arises.

Genesis 3:14-15 - "And the Lord God said unto the serpent, Because thou hast done this, thou art cursed above all cattle, and above every beast of the field; upon thy belly shalt thou go, and dust shalt thou eat all the days of thy life: And I will put enmity between thee and the woman, and between thy seed and her seed; it shall bruise thy head, and thou shalt bruise his heel" (**KJV**).

The word enmity means hatred or opposition, and what we find is a simple hatred or opposition between those that behave like the serpent and the seed of the woman, which here is ultimately the promise of the Lord Jesus Christ, who is the perfect example of someone who put the mind of God into action, and in our reading, Paul uses the phrase "the mind of Christ". Those who have the mind of Christ will be in constant opposition with the way of the serpent (Editor, 2019).

In **Matthew 3**, John the Baptist while addressing the Pharisees and the Sadducees, he calls them a brood of vipers. In **Matthew 23**, Jesus calls the Scribes and Pharisees, serpents and a brood of vipers, they obviously weren't snakes, but in other words they were behaving like the serpent, or the offspring of the serpent that was to bruise the offspring of the woman. This serpentine thinking is used often throughout the Bible as a symbol of sin and helps us to understand that wanting to do the things of the serpent is natural thinking.

So we have God's way of thinking, and this snakelike way of thinking, and there is this battle between the two. Man naturally will think like the serpent, not like God. Paul uses this symbol and describes it as carnal thinking, our word carnal is derived from the Latin word for flesh. It's this kind of animal thinking that man will naturally tend towards; an animal thinks of not much more than reproducing, where its next meal will come from, and perhaps some play; if you have pets like cats or dogs you'll understand.

That sums up many human beings, but God has made mankind differently because he has given them the ability to rise above basic animal thoughts and lift up our minds to higher things. God has given us the ability to think on spiritual things, the things that God wants us to consider. And there is the difference, this natural desire to think like an animal but with the ability to overcome that natural fleshly way of thinking. How do we even start to overcome our natural thinking though? It does come naturally to us after all. Paul wrote of that very problem.

Romans 7:14-25 - "So the trouble is not with the law, for it is spiritual and good. The trouble is with me, for I am all too human, a slave to sin. I don't really understand myself, for I want to do what is right, but I don't do it. Instead, I do what I hate. But if I know that what I am doing is wrong, this shows that I agree that the law is good. So I am not the one doing wrong; it is sin living in me that does it. And I know that nothing good lives in me, that is, in my sinful nature. I want to do what is right, but I can't. I want to do what is good, but I don't. I don't want to do what is wrong, but I do it anyway. But if I do what I don't want to do, I am not really the one doing wrong; it is sin living in me that does it. I have discovered this principle of life that when I want to do what is right, I inevitably do what is wrong. I love God's law with all my heart. But there is another power within me that is at war with my mind. This power makes me a slave to the sin that is still within me. Oh, what a miserable person I am! Who will free me from this life that is dominated by sin and death? Thank God! The answer is in Jesus Christ our Lord. So you see how it is: In my mind I really want to obey God's law, but because of my sinful nature I am a slave to sin" (**NLT**).

This is a great description of the battle that goes on within our own bodies, the natural thinking of man at war with the thinking of God. If we let the mind of God enter into our lives then it will begin to push out the things that we naturally want to do. We have to understand that God's ways are very different to our own natural ways and the ways of God won't just happen within us because they are simply not in our nature. We see a good illustration of the two types of thinking in **Genesis 4** and the example of Cain and Abel.

Genesis 4:3-5 - "When it was time for the harvest, Cain presented some of his crops as a gift to the LORD. Abel also brought a gift—the best portions of the firstborn lambs from his flock. The LORD accepted Abel and his gift, but he did not accept Cain and his gift. This made Cain very angry, and he looked dejected" (**NLT**).

To understand why God liked Abel's offering but not Cain's we have to go back a chapter.

Genesis 3:21 - "And the Lord God made clothing from animal skins for Adam and his wife" (**NLT**).

God made coats of animal skins for Adam and Eve, God was showing man how he wanted worship to be done and what was acceptable to him, and this was even mentioned in the New Testament even though it happened thousands of years before.

Hebrews 11:4 - "It was by faith that Abel brought a more acceptable offering to God than Cain did. Abel's offering gave evidence that he was a righteous man, and God showed his approval of his gifts. Although Abel is long dead, he still speaks to us by his example of faith" (**NLT**).

Here God is telling us that there is a specific way to come to him, and that was through the sacrifice of animals, until the sacrifice of Christ that is, which was the perfect sacrifice once and for all. Abel applies that godly thinking and presents God with an acceptable sacrifice; while Cain does what he thinks is best and applies his human thinking. We then see a graphic example of the enmity that exists between the two types of thinking, with Cain rising up and slaying his brother.

Even the whole concept of man's thinking is twisted by man's thinking. We are constantly taught by the world that there are good people with a few bad people thrown in, but man is basically good; that is opposite to what the Bible tells us. Look at this verse from the prophecy of Jeremiah.

Jeremiah 17:9 - "The human heart is the most deceitful of all things, and desperately wicked. Who really knows how bad it is" (**NLT**)?

Man thinks that the heart is generally good and sometimes it goes bad, but that's the opposite to what God says. We have to have the basic understanding that the Bible clearly tells us that man is not basically good, but rather man is bad. That might sound a bit depressing, God is saying that we are not good, but there is a reason why he wants us to understand that (Editor, 2019).

I Corinthians 2:12-16 - "And we have received God's Spirit (not the world's spirit), so we can know the wonderful things God has freely given us. When we tell you these things, we do not use words that come from human wisdom. Instead, we speak words given to us by the Spirit, using the Spirit's words to explain spiritual truths. But people who aren't spiritual can't receive these truths from God's Spirit. It all sounds foolish to them and they can't understand it, for only those who are spiritual can understand what the Spirit means. Those who are spiritual can evaluate all things, but they themselves cannot be evaluated by others. For, "Who can know the LORD's thoughts? Who knows enough to teach him?" But we understand these things, for we have the mind of Christ" (**NLT**).

What God says is true, the natural mind is naturally separate from God and God's ideas are alien to man. The natural man is not able to understand them because only the spiritual mind can make any sense of them. The development of a spiritual mind is not something that can happen overnight. Thinking like God is not natural. In much the same way you won't learn to play the piano, or drive a car, or learn to read overnight, it takes time and it takes guidance from someone who knows what they are doing to show you.

It's only by allowing God to show us his spiritual mind and the constant application of his ways will we begin to develop a spiritual mind and affect the natural way of thinking. We can do this by reading the Bible, absorbing the words of God, and thinking upon the man who is described as the word made flesh, that of course is the Son of God, Jesus Christ. We need to think about what he said, what he did, how he acted, and how everything thing he did was all about his Father in heaven. Every single thing he did or said was declaring his Father, he put God's thinking within himself, as God breathed out his word, Jesus breathed it all in.

The knowledge of worldly things is no use to us in understanding the things of God and it is only by reading and absorbing the word of God that we develop a spiritual mind able to understand all the things freely given to us by God. It's only by having the mind of Christ (who had the mind of his Father), will we overcome the fleshly person and become that spiritual person, and how do we know if we are putting God's word into our minds?

Galatians 5 shows us how we can judge whether our thinking is that of men or God's:

Galatians 5:17-23 - "The sinful nature wants to do evil, which is just the opposite of what the Spirit wants. And the Spirit gives us desires that are the opposite of what the sinful nature desires. These two forces are constantly fighting each other, so you are not free to carry out your good intentions. But when you are directed by the Spirit, you are not under obligation to the law of Moses. When you follow the desires of your sinful nature, the results are very clear: sexual immorality, impurity, lustful pleasures, idolatry, sorcery, hostility, quarreling, jealousy, outbursts of anger, selfish ambition, dissension, division, envy, drunkenness, wild parties, and other sins like these. Let me tell you again, as I have before, that anyone living that sort of life will not inherit the Kingdom of God. But the Holy Spirit produces this kind of fruit in our lives: love, joy, peace, patience, kindness, goodness, faithfulness, gentleness, and self-control. There is no law against these things" (**NLT**).

There are nine virtues called the fruit of the spirit, and 15 bad things, or 17 in the KJV. If we are of a spiritual mind then those good things are what we will do naturally, and if we have the mind of the natural man then we will be doing the bad things naturally. We should hopefully see that spiritual mind in action. We don't do those good works to gain a spiritual mind, we do them because we already have a spiritual mind (Editor, 2019).

Romans 8:5 - "Those who are dominated by the sinful nature think about sinful things, but those who are controlled by the Holy Spirit think about things that please the Spirit" (**NLT**).

Where do we put our time and energy? Do we spend more time thinking about the things of the flesh, or do we spend more time on God's word and the application of it in our lives? Whatever you do, it will be seen by your fruit, whether it be the fruit of the spirit, or the fruit of the flesh. Where we get into difficulties though is when we think it is okay to mix the two, for they cannot live together in harmony, they are opposite to each other. We've already said that there is an enmity between them. We have to put in a lot of spiritual to overcome the natural flesh.

One of the most difficult things to overcome with man's thinking is being stuck in the present, rather than thinking like God and thinking beyond to the future kingdom. We can get stuck with all the human activities that take up our time, the lusts and pleasures of the world. We can get bogged down with trying to acquire possessions, or money, or worldly status.

I Timothy 6:7-8 - "After all, we brought nothing with us when we came into the world, and we can't take anything with us when we leave it. So if we have enough food and clothing, let us be content" (NLT).

That's completely opposite to worldly thinking. The world bombards us with marketing telling us that unless we have the newest, the biggest and the best we will never be happy. But God says,

Matthew 6:33 - "Seek the Kingdom of God above all else, and live righteously, and he will give you everything you need" (NLT).

Seek the kingdom of God first, not second, and then whatever else is deemed necessary will be added. We can really see the difference between the mind of God and the mind of man here. The natural eyes of man sees a beautiful Ferrari or Lamborghini and it sees a magnificent mansion. It sees a high flying executive job with an office at the top of a wonderful skyscraper and it sees endless holidays on a hot sunny Mediterranean beach. I'm sure you can think of many other things too. Do you know what the spiritual eyes see? Nothing. That's right. Nothing.

II Corinthians 4:18 - "So we don't look at the troubles we can see now; rather, we fix our gaze on things that cannot be seen. For the things we see now will soon be gone, but the things we cannot see will last forever" (**NLT**).

The spiritual mind sees nothing in this world. That's because the spiritual mind doesn't look to the things of this world, but to the things that can't be seen. No-one here has seen God, or Jesus or the kingdom, no-one knows what they look like, yet the spiritual mind believes that God exists and that His son Jesus will return to the earth to set up his Father's kingdom. We have never seen them but the spiritual mind knows they are real.

The flesh says that all the things we see around us are real; it only believes in the things it can see. The spiritual mind says the things that we can't see are real. So, how do we think like God? By walking in the spirit, by reading God's word and studying it, and spending time with other people who are studying it. When we do this the spiritual seed will grow within us, we will start to recognize the natural thinking within us and that seed will grow and produce fruit.

We are very much like a house plant. After the seed is planted in the soil, at first it will do nothing, but when start to read God's word it's like pouring water into that pot. The seed starts to grow and develop. But we must keep pouring the water or the Word of God onto that seedling to keep it growing. It's that water that helps us to grow, and without it we will die, but keep on watering little and often and the seedling will become a fruit bearing plant, water too much and the excess will run off and be wasted. Developing a spiritual mind doesn't happen overnight, it takes time and patience, you can't pour the whole Word of God over someone and expect them to absorb it all at once!

However, we can't take any credit for any of the good fruit that we produce because it comes from God, it's by taking in that Word of God we develop a spiritual mind and bear fruit. I'm sure you've all experienced the joy of looking after a potted plant at home, and if you've remembered to water it, watching it produce its lovely flowers or fruit. It wasn't the plant's choice to produce that fruit, it had no say in the matter, you giving it water made it bear fruit, all the plant had to do was be willing to absorb that water through its roots and then it will naturally grow towards the light. The same is true with us, we have to be willing to absorb the Word of God and let it help us grow.

Jeremiah 17:7-8 - "But blessed are those who trust in the LORD and have made the LORD their hope and confidence. They are like trees planted along a riverbank, with roots that reach deep into the water. Such trees are not bothered by the heat or worried by long months of drought. Their leaves stay green, and they never stop producing fruit" (**NLT**).

This is a very powerful image, for the man who drinks continuously from the Word of God will have nothing to fear. When things get difficult in life that water will keep the tree healthy and bearing fruit, but all the tree had to do was search out the water. The rest came naturally. When Jesus was called good teacher, he replied, "Why do you call me good? No-one is good except God alone". Jesus gave his Father the credit due because the Word of God came from God and Jesus allowed himself to be filled with it. Jesus was a vessel for God's word, and it was that word that made him think like his Father, not the nature of Jesus himself for he was given the same nature as we are.

To develop and bear the fruit of the spirit we must seek the guidance of God and drink from the spiritual well of God's word. Jesus tells us the same in the New Testament.

John 4:14 - "But those who drink the water I give will never be thirsty again. It becomes a fresh, bubbling spring within them, giving them eternal life" (**NLT**).

That's what Jesus had promised to those who follow him and think like him. Finally come back to our opening verse that we looked at, the one I asked you to keep in mind throughout this talk.

Isaiah 55:8-9 - "My thoughts are nothing like your thoughts," says the LORD. "And my ways are far beyond anything you could imagine. For just as the heavens are higher than the earth, so my ways are higher than your ways and my thoughts higher than your thoughts" (**NLT**).

We have discovered that our ways are indeed not God's ways, they are certainly higher than our thoughts, and there is no way that God will come down to our level. However we have also discovered that although we can't change the nature of the flesh, we can leave our natural ways of thinking behind but only if we let God's Word permeate through our minds so that his ways of thinking take over. So let us allow the Word of God to water our minds and allow it to work in our lives to help us grow in our spiritual thinking and put on the mind of Christ.

Seek the kingdom of God first and then whatever else is deemed necessary will be added.

Man cannot save himself because of how he thinks.

CHAPTER 3

MIND OVER MATTER

The phrase *mind over matter* is typically used as a motivation to overcome difficult obstacles: the idea is that, if you put your mind to it, you can do anything. Of course, there are limitations to this encouragement, including the laws of nature. No matter how much a person "believes" he can fly by flapping his arms, the laws of nature will prove otherwise. Reality has a way of intruding (Henriques, 2011).

Some people try to apply the concept of "mind over matter" to Scripture in an attempt to explain some of the events recorded there. For example, some might say that, when Peter walked on water for a short distance to go to Jesus, who was also walking on the water.

Matthew 14:22-23 - "Then he made the disciples get into the boat and go before him to the other side, while he dismissed the crowds. And after he had dismissed the crowds, he went up on the mountain by himself to pray. When evening came, he was there alone" **(RSV)**.

Peter was able to do so because Jesus was teaching him to put mind over matter. It's true that Peter walked on water, but it had nothing to do with "mind over matter."

The Bible does not countenance the idea of mind over matter. There is nothing in Scripture to support the idea that the human mind has the power to overcome the laws of nature or that our minds can exert an observable influence over the material world. The Bible gives plenty of examples of *God's* mind over matter, but not *our* minds. In **Matthew 14**, Jesus walked on the water of the Sea of Galilee as a display of His own supernatural power. When His disciples saw Him, they did not say, "Look at His mental powers!"

Peter asked for the ability to walk on the water to Jesus to confirm it was really Jesus: "Lord, if it's you, . . . tell me to come to you on the water"

Matthew 14:28 - "And Peter answered him, "Lord, if it is you, bid me come to you on the water" (**RSV**).

Jesus told Peter to come and, in so doing, gave Peter the ability to do so. Peter took several steps on the water toward the Lord. But then he began to fear the waves and the wind, and he began to sink. Jesus caught Peter before he sank and then questioned Peter's doubting faith. The problem that led to Peter's sinking was not a lack of confidence in his own mind but a lack of faith in the Lord who was sustaining him.

When the two men got back in the boat, the winds died down, and everyone in the boat worshipped Jesus, saying, "Truly you are the Son of God".

Matthew 14:33 - "And those in the boat worshiped him, saying, "Truly you are the Son of God" (**RSV**).

This is a significant detail. No one praised Peter for his ability to put mind over matter; everyone praised Jesus for demonstrating who He was. Walking on the water was no mental feat; it was the supernatural power of God at work.

Skeptics often seek to attribute acts of the supernatural to acts of nature, giving "logical" human explanations for what the Bible calls miracles. The idea of "mind over matter" can't really be called a "logical" explanation, but at least it avoids having to acknowledge God, and some skeptics will use it, too. Of course, those who claim that Peter walked on water due to his own mental strength fail to provide experiential evidence of someone today accomplishing the same action. There is no person alive today who is walking on water and saying it is due to his or her mind powers. The only people ever to walk on water are Jesus and Peter, the Son of God and the one He had specifically told to come to Him (Henriques, 2011).

In **Acts 3**, Peter and John healed a man who had been unable to walk since he was born.

Acts 3:2 - "And a man lame from birth was being carried, whom they laid daily at that gate of the temple which is called Beautiful to ask alms of those who entered the temple" (**RSV**).

After the healing, a crowd began to gather, and Peter explained what had happened: "By faith in the name of Jesus, this man whom you see and know was made strong. It is Jesus' name and the faith that comes through him that has completely healed him, as you can all see"

Acts 3:16 - "And his name, by faith in his name, has made this man strong whom you see and know; and the faith which is through Jesus has given the man this perfect health in the presence of you all" (**RSV**).

In other words, the lame man did not practice "mind over matter" and so overcome his disability; it was faith in Jesus Christ that healed him. The object of our faith is not our minds; it is the Lord Jesus. The Creator of the universe can speak things into existence or change the course of nature with a thought. We don't have that power. Simply "putting your mind to it," focusing on an object and telling it to "move," or thinking "mind over matter" does not negate reality. We have limitations. Only God has the power to overcome our limitations, even in impossible situations, when we are trusting Him to accomplish His will.

Truly you are the Son of God!

CHAPTER 4

OVER THINKING

When you think too much, instead of acting and doing things, you are overthinking. When you analyze, comment and repeat the same thoughts over and again, instead of acting, you are overthinking.

They overthink every little problem until it becomes bigger and scarier than it actually is. They overthink positive things until they don't look so positive anymore. Continuously thinking on events of the past and what may lie ahead of us in the future can paralyse our normal thought process and lead to inaction or incorrect action in the present. It affects us mentally, physically and emotionally.

It is your life, and you get one shot at it. Don't waste it by whiling away on trivial matters. Take action and regain control of your thoughts. One way to avoid over-thinking a subject is to incorporate Scripture and prayer into one's thoughts. The psalmists states:

Psalm 94:19 - "When anxiety was great within me, your consolation brought me joy" (**NIV**).

Many of the **Psalms** were written by over thinkers who were facing danger, emotional unrest, fear, or despair. They boldly wrote out their anxious thoughts and then turned them into the worship of God.

Psalm 6:1-10 - "Lord, do not rebuke me in your anger or discipline me in your wrath. 2 Have mercy on me, Lord, for I am faint; heal me, Lord, for my bones are in agony. 3 My soul is in deep anguish. How long, Lord, how long? 4 Turn, Lord, and deliver me; save me because of your unfailing love. 5 Among the dead no one proclaims your name. Who praises you from the grave? 6 I am worn out from my groaning. All night long I flood my bed with weeping and drench my couch with tears. 7 My eyes grow weak with sorrow; they fail because of all my foes. 8 Away from me, all you who do evil, for the Lord has heard my weeping. 9 The Lord has heard my cry for mercy; the Lord accepts my prayer. 10 All my enemies will be overwhelmed with shame and anguish; they will turn back and suddenly be put to shame" (**NIV**).

Verse 6 describes the condition of many who overthink: "I am worn out from my groaning. All night long I flood my bed with weeping and drench my couch with tears." Yet the author, David, does not stop there. The psalm ends with these words: "The Lord has heard my cry for mercy; the Lord accepts my prayer. All my enemies will be overwhelmed with shame and anguish; they will turn back and suddenly be put to shame" (**verses 9–10**).

Satan capitalizes on our inclination to overthink by creating uncertainty and fear about our salvation and spirituality. Some Christians who overthink have difficulty resting in their salvation because they over-analyze their grace-based relationship with God and do not rest in "the simplicity that is in Christ".

II Corinthians 11:3 - "But I am afraid that just as Eve was deceived by the serpent's cunning, your minds may somehow be led astray from your sincere and pure devotion to Christ" (**NIV**).

They fear that, if they haven't thought of everything, God might reject them. This is unhealthy and an example of the fiery darts warned about in:

Ephesians 6:16 - "In addition to all this, take up the shield of faith, with which you can extinguish all the flaming arrows of the evil one" (**NIV**).

Overthinking and worrying tricks our brains into believing that we are preparing for every situation, that we can handle any outcome, positive or negative. In reality, while this may work in the short-term, it ultimately harms us. Try to notice when you are overthinking and doubting yourself and stop yourself at that very moment. The problems with overthinking? It's useless, and it's exhausting. You wear yourself out over it, and it doesn't get you anywhere.

Trust me, if you are worried that you might be doing something wrong, you are probably doing everything right except worrying about what you are doing wrong. Over-thinking leads to blame, one way or the other, you or them. Stop the blame cycle! If you tend toward overthinking, know yourself, know your tendencies, but most of all, know the truth: Jesus died for your what if anxieties, and he won't let you fall into despair when you cling to his precious promises.

Philippians 4:6-7 - "Do not be anxious about anything, but in every situation, by prayer and petition, with thanksgiving, present your requests to God. And the peace of God, which transcends all understanding, will guard your hearts and your minds in Christ Jesus" (**NIV**).

A full life doesn't mean full of crippling thoughts and fear. **I John 4:18,** (**NIV**), says that "perfect love drives out fear". The cool thing about that is that it's not about how perfect we are – it's how perfect God's love is for us. It is vital to implant in our consciousness that there is a Creator, a basic awareness of the presence of God in our lives. As it says in Psalms: I keep my eyes always on the LORD. With him at my right hand, I will not be shaken" (**Psalms 16:8**).

Avoid overthinking by incorporating Scripture and Prayer into your thoughts.

CHAPTER 5

TAKE EVERY THOUGHT CAPTIVE

In speaking of our spiritual warfare, Paul says that we take every thought captive and subject all thinking to Christ Jesus. Here are the apostle's words:

II Corinthians 10:5 - "We demolish arguments and every pretension that sets itself up against the knowledge of God, and we take captive every thought to make it obedient to Christ" (**NIV**).

The primary point in this section of II Corinthians is that we are in a spiritual warfare. What leads up to the statement that we take every thought captive is important. In **verse 3** Paul states that though we walk in the flesh we do not war after the flesh. That is, we do not rely on human ingenuity or man made plans to bring the victory. The flesh is powerless against the wiles of the devil. In **verse 4** Paul mentions the "strongholds" or the "fortresses" that are destroyed by God's power. These strongholds are the philosophies, arguments, and "proud opinions" mentioned in **verse 5** (Ganz, 2000).

Without question, there are many human thoughts that need to be taken captive. Numerous ungodly philosophies hold people in bondage, and those spiritual "fortresses" need to be demolished. The systems of thought that war against us are "arrogant obstacles" (**NET**), "lofty opinions" (**ESV**), and "sophisticated arguments and every exalted and proud thing" (**AMP**) that prevent people from knowing God. In our day, these systems of human thought include the theory of evolution, secular humanism, existentialism, the cults, the occult, and false religions. How many people are held captive by the idea that they are the products of chance in a godless universe? How many spiritual prisoners labor under the requirements of Allah and await freedom in Christ? We must take captive every thought and make it obedient to Christ. "If the Son sets you free, you will be free indeed" (Ganz, 2000).

John 8:36 - "So if the Son sets you free, you will be free indeed" (**NIV**).

False religion and secular philosophy have created thinking that has imprisoned the minds of millions. It is a true spiritual battle:

II Corinthians 4:4 - "The god of this age has blinded the minds of unbelievers, so that they cannot see the light of the gospel that displays the glory of Christ, who is the image of God" (**NIV**).

Any idea, opinion, or worldview that asserts that Christ is unnecessary is reflective of the devil's pride. Such thoughts must be taken captive and made obedient to Christ. Those who know the truth must confront error with the weapon we've been given, the sword of the Spirit, which is the Word of God.

Ephesians 6:17 - "Take the helmet of salvation and the sword of the Spirit, which is the word of God" (**NIV**).

Our weapons in the spiritual battle are not carnal but mighty through God. As we are transformed by the renewing of our minds:

Romans 12:2 - "Do not conform to the pattern of this world, but be transformed by the renewing of your mind. Then you will be able to test and approve what God's will is, his good, pleasing and perfect will" (**NIV**).

We engage the battle against pretense and arrogant philosophy in the world. Trusting Christ and rightly dividing the Word of God.

II Timothy 2:15 - "Do your best to present yourself to God as one approved, a worker who does not need to be ashamed and who correctly handles the word of truth" (NIV).

We take every thought captive, pull down the strongholds, and, by the grace of God, set the captives free. By the Holy Spirit we can get grace and power to bring the thoughts into captivity to the obedience of Christ, and in this process, we become transformed into the person He wants us to be. We have the wonderful hope that by overcoming sin in our thought life, we can become a little more like Christ as each day progresses. In this way, we become valuable tools in God's hands. Allowing this inner work of God to take place in us is the greatest task we can take on in life.

Our weapons in the spiritual battle are not carnal.

CHAPTER 6

CONTROLLING MY THOUGHTS

Maybe you don't have any trouble with your thoughts, but I do. Thoughts pop into my mind without my permission. Many Christians struggle with their thought "life". In our highly technological world, but taking control of our thoughts becomes more difficult.

Proverbs 4:23 - "Watch over your heart with all diligence, For from it *flow* the springs of life" (**NASB**).

The passage states, "Above all else, guard your heart, for it is the wellspring of life." The "heart" includes the mind and all that proceeds from it. The fact that you and I can think, reflect on the past, imagine the future, is what distinguishes humans from all other animals.

There is also a difference between being tempted, a thought entering into the mind, and sinning, dwelling upon an evil thought. It is important to understand that when a thought enters our mind, we examine it based upon God's Word and determine if we should continue down that path or reject the thought. James said, that every man is tempted, when he is drawn away of his own lust, and enticed (**James 1:14, KJV**). If we have already allowed sinful thought to form and dwell in our mind, it becomes more difficult to change the path of our thoughts. Here are some biblical suggestions for taking control of our thoughts and getting rid of wrong thoughts:

1. *Meditate daily.* You CAN learn to meditate and you must, if you wish to learn to control your thoughts and your thinking.

Joshua 1:8 - "Keep this Book of the Law always on your lips; meditate on it day and night, so that you may be careful to do everything written in it. Then you will be prosperous and successful" (**NIV**).

Jesus in the wilderness in Matthew 4 responded to each of Satan's temptations with Scripture that applied to the direction He knew His mind should take instead of beginning down the path of the sinful thought. When tempted to meet His physical need (turn stone into bread), He recited the passage about the importance of relying upon God. When tempted to test God (to see if God was really there and would keep His promises), Jesus responded with passages that stress the importance of believing God without having to see Him demonstrate His presence (Goldstein, 2018).

Quoting Scripture in a time of temptation serves the purpose of getting our minds onto a biblical track, but we need to know the Word of God. We need to study and memorize key passages of the bible that deal with our issues. How we properly respond to tempting thoughts and situations, before they are upon us will go a long way to giving us victory over them.

2. *Inventory your thoughts daily as you reflect on the day.*

Matthew 26:41 - "Keep watching and praying that you may not enter into temptation; the spirit is willing, but the flesh is weak" (**NASB**).

Jesus says, "Stop Doing Things in your own Strength".

Proverbs 28:26 - "He who trusts in his own heart is a fool, But he who walks wisely will be delivered" (**NASB**).

> "I'm not good enough."
>
> "I'm going to fail."
>
> "He doesn't really like me."
>
> "Something's wrong with me."

Have you ever been haunted by thoughts like that? Perhaps you don't even recognize how often you have those thoughts because they are a permanent transcript in your brain. Be careful of the thoughts that you are feeding your brain.

Jeremiah 17:9 - "The heart is more deceitful than all else And is desperately sick; Who can understand it" (**NASB**)?

Matthew 26:33 - "But Peter said to Him, *'Even* though all may fall away because of You, I will never fall away'" (**NASB**).

When I realized that I could change my thoughts and the quality of my life, the first thing I did was begin to become aware of how I talked to myself by taking a thought inventory.

3. *Train and Renew your mind daily* - "By the renewal of your mind" - (**Romans 12:2, KJV**).

Don't doubt the power of your mind. This football-sized mass has the power to create and recreate everything in your life. "Your Mind Is Renewed To The Degree That It Dictates Your Daily Actions!"

This is why Jesus tells us not to conform to the pattern of the world, but be transformed by the renewing of our mind. If we renew our mind, it is like getting a re-do on life

Romans 13:14 - "But put on the Lord Jesus Christ, and make no provision for the flesh in regard to its lusts" (**NASB**).

You must speak God's truth to the evil thoughts that come to you. "This is a temptation from Satan to get me to lie, or to lust, or whatever the thought focuses on. And here is what God says about that issue"-and then you need to remind yourself of the specific truth that relates to that evil thought. When evil thoughts come into your mind, don't try to run from them-attack them! Use the tools God has given you. Once you have exposed what you are battling, then begin to focus on the positive things God speaks of and bring God into the battle.

4. *We are to seek after the things of God.*

Colossians 3:1-4 - "Therefore if you have been raised up with Christ, keep seeking the things above, where Christ is, seated at the right hand of God. Set your mind on the things above, not on the things that are on earth. For you have died and your life is hidden with Christ in God. When Christ, who is our life, is revealed, then you also will be revealed with Him in glory" (**NASB**).

For example: **II Chronicles 15** was written over two thousand years ago to a people like us.

II Chronicles 15:2-4 - "And he went out to meet Asa and said to him, "Listen to me, Asa, and all Judah and Benjamin: the Lord is with you when you are with Him. And if you seek Him, He will let you find Him; but if you forsake Him, He will forsake you. For many days Israel was without the true God and without a teaching priest and without law. But in their distress they turned to the Lord God of Israel, and they sought Him, and He let them find Him" (**NASB**).

Their instructions were simple: when they sincerely sought God, things went well, but when their desire to seek Him waned and eventually ceased altogether, their world came apart. Sin increased, morality declined, contact with God ceased. The idea is that when we draw near to God, He reveals Himself to us. God does not hide Himself from the seeking heart.

Matthew 5:44 - "But I say to you, love your enemies and pray for those who persecute you" (**NASB**).

We all experience times in our lives when we are persecuted by our family members, friends, colleagues, bosses and others. Even though this persecution may persist for a long time, instead of retaliating as they expect and want you to, take it to the Lord in prayer. Let the Lord fight your battles for you. This prayer can be used daily as you surrender all to our Lord and Savior, Jesus Christ. No weapon formed against me shall prosper. You, Lord, are all powerful and almighty. And despite the situation I'm in, I place my trust in you.

Ephesians 4:28 - "He who steals must steal no longer; but rather he must labor, performing with his own hands what is good, so that he will have *something* to share with one who has need" (**NASB**).

The Bible often speaks of "putting off" wrong actions and thoughts but then "putting on" Godly actions and thoughts.

Ephesians 4:22-32 - "That, in reference to your former manner of life, you lay aside the old self, which is being corrupted in accordance with the lusts of deceit, and that you be renewed in the spirit of your mind, and put on the new self, which [cin *the likeness of* God has been created in righteousness and holiness of the truth. Therefore, laying aside falsehood, SPEAK TRUTH EACH ONE *of you* WITH HIS NEIGHBOR, for we are members of one another. BE ANGRY, AND *yet* DO NOT SIN; do not let the sun go down on your anger, and do not give the devil an opportunity. He who steals must steal no longer; but rather he must labor, performing with his own hands what is good, so that he will have *something* to share with one who has need. Let no unwholesome word proceed from your mouth, but only such *a word* as is good for edification according to the need *of the moment*, so that it will give grace to those who hear. Do not grieve the Holy

Spirit of God, by whom you were sealed for the day of redemption. Let all bitterness and wrath and anger and clamor and slander be put away from you, along with all malice. Be kind to one another, tenderhearted, forgiving each other, just as God in Christ also has forgiven you" (**NASB**).

Merely seeking to put off sinful thoughts is not enough. We must be filled with His spirit and strong in the word. Once we are clean in areas of our life those places must be filled. Otherwise as the Bible says Satan will fill them and he will be 7 times stronger in us than before.

Matthew 12:43-45 - "Now when the unclean spirit goes out of a man, it passes through waterless places seeking rest, and does not find it. Then it says, 'I will return to my house from which I came'; and when it comes, it finds it unoccupied, swept, and put in order. Then it goes and takes along with it seven other spirits more wicked than itself, and they go in and live there; and the last state of that man becomes worse than the first. That is the way it will also be with this evil generation" (**NASB**).

5. *Fellowship with believers*

Hebrews 10:24-25 - "And let us consider how to stimulate one another to love and good deeds, not forsaking our own assembling together, as is the habit of some, but encouraging *one another*; and all the more as you see the day drawing near" (**NASB**).

This passage says to not give up meeting together but let us encourage one another and all the more as you see the Day approaching. Fellow Christians who can encourage us in the changes we desire, who will pray for and with us, who will ask us how we are doing, and who will hold us accountable in avoiding the old ways, are valuable friends indeed.

Last and most important, these methods will be of no value unless we have placed our faith in Christ as Savior from our sin. This is where we absolutely must start! Without this, there can be no victory over sinful thoughts and temptations, God's promises for His children will be null, and the power of the Holy Spirit will not be ours.

God will bless those who seek to honor Him with what matters most to Him: who we are inside and not just what we appear to be to others. May God make Jesus' description of Nathaniel true also of us, a man or woman in whom there is no guile.

John 1:47 - "Jesus saw Nathaniel coming to Him, and said of him, 'Behold, an Israelite indeed, in whom there is no deceit'" (**NASB**)!

Your mind is like a garden that needs a good daily care. Your mind is like a garden and you are the gardener general. Your body is a vessel that carries your soul, so you must take good care of it

> "Even though nothing lasts forever, you can extend the longevity of things with positive actions, regular maintenance, and constant growth and improvement. Your body and mind are no exceptions to that. With regular maintenance, they both last longer and function better. That's exactly what you want" (Blaz, 2017).

Your mind can become your best friend or your worst enemy. It can also be your biggest supporter or biggest adversary. The choice *is* yours!

Above all else, guard your heart, for it is the wellspring of life.

CHAPTER 7

NEGATIVE THINKING

C hronic negative thinking, depression, anxiety, and similar disorders are on the rise all over the world. According to the Anxiety and Depression Association of America, 40 million adults in the U.S. are affected, which is nearly 20 percent of the population. Of that number, many are professing Christians (Ellis, 2015).

Fear seems to be a root cause of many of these problems. It's no wonder people are fearful in a world where it appears nothing is reliable. It can be quite disturbing for a person to realize almost everything in life is ultimately out of his control from the weather to his bank account balance. All the things people rely on for their security will sooner or later fail them. But the Christian who confesses the sovereignty of an Almighty God who works all things for his good,

Romans 8:28 - "And we know that God causes all things to work together for good to those who love God, to those who are called according to *His* purpose" (**NASB**).

This verse has the antidote to negative thinking.

When a Christian's thinking is primarily negative, anxious, or doubtful, it's a sign of a serious lack of faith. The author of Hebrews states, "Without faith it is impossible to please God".

Hebrews 11:6 - "And without faith it is impossible to please *Him*, for he who comes to God must believe that He is and *that* He is a rewarder of those who seek Him" (**NASB**).

And, according to:

Proverbs 29:25 - "The fear of man brings a snare, But he who trusts in the LORD will be exalted" (**NASB**).

Fear is a trap but trust in the Lord keeps a man safe. Jesus, when boating with His disciples during a terrible storm, asked them, "You of little faith, why are you so afraid?"

Matthew 8:26 - "He said to them, "Why are you afraid, you men of little faith?" Then He got up and rebuked the winds and the sea, and it became perfectly calm" (**NASB**).

Those who struggle with negative thinking should do the same thing they would do with any other sin, confess it (agree with God that negative thinking is wrong because it reveals a lack of trust) and make every effort to change the behavior.

Prayer is a key part of overcoming negativity. Jesus taught that prayer should include praise to the Father and a focus on His holiness (Ellis, 2015).

Matthew 6:9 - "Pray, then, in this way: Our Father who is in heaven, Hallowed be Your name" (**NASB**).

Psalm 95:2 - "Let us come before His presence with thanksgiving, Let us shout joyfully to Him with psalms" (**NASB**).

As we pray "with thanksgiving":

Philippians 4:6 - "Be anxious for nothing, but in everything by prayer and supplication with thanksgiving let your requests be made known to God" (**NASB**).

We focus on the blessings we have received and leave no room for negative thoughts. The Holy Spirit will be faithful to help the repentant believer overcome negative thinking.

Matthew 7:7-11 - "Ask, and it will be given to you; seek, and you will find; knock, and it will be opened to you. For everyone who asks receives, and he who seeks finds, and to him who knocks it will be opened. Or what man is there among you who, when his son asks for a loaf, will give him a stone? Or if he asks for a fish, he will not give him a snake, will he? If you then, being evil, know how to give good gifts to your children, how much more will your Father who is in heaven give what is good to those who ask Him" (**NASB**)!

Daily Bible reading, particularly studies that focus on the promises of God, are of great help in overcoming negative thinking. It's helpful to remember that, no matter how dismal the present circumstances, Christians have been promised God's love and victory in Christ

Romans 8:37-39 - "But in all these things we overwhelmingly conquer through Him who loved us. For I am convinced that neither death, nor life, nor angels, nor principalities, nor things present, nor things to come, nor powers, nor height, nor depth, nor any other created thing, will be able to separate us from the love of God, which is in Christ Jesus our Lord" (**NASB**).

II Corinthians 2:14 - "But thanks be to God, who in Christ always leads us in triumph, and through us spreads the fragrance of the knowledge of him everywhere" (**RSV**).

The Scriptures are bursting with admonitions from God to His people to overcome fear and doubt, over 350 commands to "fear not." As a matter of fact, the one verbal encouragement Jesus gives more than any other is a call to fearless living (Ellis, 2015).

Matthew 6:25 - "Therefore I tell you, do not be anxious about your life, what you shall eat or what you shall drink, nor about your body, what you shall put on. Is not life more than food, and the body more than clothing" (**RSV**)?

Matthew 9:2 - "And behold, they brought to him a paralytic, lying on his bed; and when Jesus saw their faith he said to the paralytic, "Take heart, my son; your sins are forgiven" (**RSV**).

Matthew 10:28 - "And do not fear those who kill the body but cannot kill the soul; rather fear him who can destroy both soul and body in hell" (**RSV**).

Matthew 10:31 - "Fear not, therefore; you are of more value than many sparrows" (**RSV**).

The struggle against negative thinking is a battle for the mind. The apostle Paul tells believers what to think about: things that are true, noble, right, pure, lovely, admirable, excellent and praiseworthy

Philippians 4:8 - "Finally, brethren, whatever is true, whatever is honorable, whatever is just, whatever is pure, whatever is lovely, whatever is gracious, if there is any excellence, if there is anything worthy of praise, think about these things" (**RSV**).

Besides defining what thoughts should fill our minds, this text implicitly teaches that we can control what we think about. When a negative thought comes, the thinker who has the mind of Christ.

I Corinthians 2:16 - "For who has known the mind of the Lord so as to instruct him?" But we have the mind of Christ" (**RSV**).

The believer has the ability to push it out of the mind and replace it with godly thoughts. This takes practice, but with persistence, it gets easier. Christians must think about what they're thinking about and not allow their minds to have free rein. In our spiritual warfare, we've been given the helmet of salvation. As long as Christians live in a fearful, stressful world, negative thoughts will come. We have the option of either stamping out those thoughts or nurturing them. The good news is, negative thoughts can be replaced with positive ones, and the more that godly substitution takes place, the more peace and joy we can experience.

Prayer is a key part of overcoming negativity.

CHAPTER 8

DOUBLE MINDED

The term *double-minded* means "a person with two minds or souls." It's interesting that this word appears only in the book of James.

James 1:8 - "Such a person is double-minded and unstable in all they do" (**NIV**).

James 4:8 - "Come near to God and he will come near to you. Wash your hands, you sinners, and purify your hearts, you double-minded" (**NIV**).

Bible scholars conclude that James might have coined this word. To grasp the full meaning of this word, it is best to understand how it is used within its context. James writes of the doubting person that he is "like a wave of the sea, blown and tossed by the wind. That man should not think he will receive anything from the Lord; he is a double-minded man, unstable in all he does" (Smith, 2016).

James 1:6-8 - "But when you ask, you must believe and not doubt, because the one who doubts is like a wave of the sea, blown and tossed by the wind. That person should not expect to receive anything from the Lord. Such a person is double-minded and unstable in all they do" (**NIV**).

A doubter is a double-minded person. Jesus had in mind such a person when He spoke of the one who tries to serve two masters.

Matthew 6:24 - "No one can serve two masters. Either you will hate the one and love the other, or you will be devoted to the one and despise the other. You cannot serve both God and money" (**NIV**).

As such, he is "unstable," which comes from a Greek word meaning "unsteady, wavering, in both his character and feelings."

A double-minded person is restless and confused in his thoughts, his actions, and his behavior. Such a person is always in conflict with himself. One torn by such inner conflict can never lean with confidence on God and His gracious promises. Correspondingly, the term *unstable* is analogous to a drunken man unable to walk a straight line, swaying one way, then another. He has no defined direction and as a result doesn't get anywhere. Such a person is "unstable in all he does" (Smith, 2016).

Those who are double-minded do not have the faith spoken of in:

Hebrews 11:1 - "Now faith is confidence in what we hope for and assurance about what we do not see" (**NIV**).

Hebrews 11:3 - "By faith we understand that the universe was formed at God's command, so that what is seen was not made out of what was visible" (**NIV**).

We cannot be both "certain" and doubting, as is the double-minded person. One part of his mind is sure of something, while the other part doubts. It brings to mind the "pushmi-pullyu" of the Dr. Doolittle stories, an animal with a head at either end of its body and which was constantly trying to walk in two directions at once. Such is the double-minded man.

Jesus declared, "No one can serve two masters. Either he will hate the one and love the other, or he will be devoted to the one and despise the other".

Matthew 6:24 - "No one can serve two masters. Either you will hate the one and love the other, or you will be devoted to the one and despise the other. You cannot serve both God and money" (**NIV**).

God and the things of this world are of such opposite natures that it is impossible to love either one completely without hating the other. Those who try to love both will become unstable in all their ways. If someone struggles with being double-minded, he or she should read, study, and memorize the Word, for it is the Word of God that produces faith.

Romans 10:17 - "Consequently, faith comes from hearing the message, and the message is heard through the word about Christ" (**NIV**).

And he or she should pray for faith. God freely gives what is good to those who ask Him.

Luke 11:9-12 - "So I say to you: Ask and it will be given to you; seek and you will find; knock and the door will be opened to you. For everyone who asks receives; the one who seeks finds; and to the one who knocks, the door will be opened. "Which of you fathers, if your son asks for a fish, will give him a snake instead? Or if he asks for an egg, will give him a scorpion" (**NIV**).

And it's good to ask for an increase of faith

Luke 17:5 - "The apostles said to the Lord, "Increase our faith" (**NIV**)!

Mark 9:24 - "Immediately the boy's father exclaimed, "I do believe; help me overcome my unbelief" (**NIV**)!

"Lord Jesus, I ask for Your forgiveness for all of the areas of my life that I have not surrendered to You, and I invite You once again to take the rightful place of Your Glory on the throne of my heart. May my life and body be a pleasing sacrifice to You. I give it to You freely. I'm all-in. Please give me the strength to do the things that I need to do and not just talk about them. In Your name I pray and give thanks."

No one can serve two masters.

CHAPTER 9

REPROBATE MIND

The phrase "reprobate mind" is in reference to those whom God has rejected as godless and wicked. They "suppress the truth by their wickedness," and it is upon these people that the wrath of God rests:

Romans 1:18 - "The wrath of God is being revealed from heaven against all the godlessness and wickedness of people, who suppress the truth by their wickedness" (**NIV**).

The Greek word translated "reprobate" in the New Testament means literally "unapproved, that is, rejected; by implication, worthless (literally or morally) (GotQuestions, 2014).

Paul describes two men named Jannes and Jambres as those who "resist the truth: men of corrupt minds, reprobate concerning the faith":

II Timothy 3:8 - "Just as Jannes and Jambres opposed Moses, so also these teachers oppose the truth. They are men of depraved minds, who, as far as the faith is concerned, are rejected" (**NIV**).

Here the reprobation is regarding the resistance to the truth because of corrupt minds. In Titus, Paul also refers to those whose works are reprobate: "They profess that they know God; but in works they deny him, being abominable, and disobedient, and unto every good work reprobate" (GotQuestions, 2014).

Titus 1:16 - "They claim to know God, but by their actions they deny him. They are detestable, disobedient and unfit for doing anything good" (**NIV**).

Therefore, the reprobate mind is one that is corrupt and worthless. As we can see in the verses above, people who are classified as having a reprobate mind have some knowledge of God and perhaps know of His commandments. However, they live impure lives and have very little desire to please God. Those who have reprobate minds live corrupt and selfish lives. Sin is justified and acceptable to them. The reprobates are those whom God has rejected and has left to their own devices.

Can a Christian have a reprobate mind? Someone who has sincerely accepted Jesus Christ by faith will not have this mindset because the old person with a reprobate mind has been recreated into a new creation: "The old has passed away; behold, the new has come"

II Corinthians 5:17 - "Therefore, if anyone is in Christ, the new creation has come: The old has gone, the new is here" (**NIV**).

Christians are basically "new" people. We live differently and speak differently. Our world is centered on our Lord and Savior, Jesus Christ, and how we can serve Him. Also, if we are truly in the faith, we will have the Holy Spirit to help us live a God-honoring life.

John 14:26 - "But the Advocate, the Holy Spirit, whom the Father will send in my name, will teach you all things and will remind you of everything I have said to you" (**NIV**).

The Reprobate Mind is one that is corrupt and worthless.

CHAPTER 10

DEPRAVED MIND

Because man turned from God to idolatry he went down instead of up; he devolved instead of evolved; and he is in the state of proceeding from bad to worse. In his downward spiral into sin man has arrived at a defiled heart (impurity), degraded passions (immorality/homosexuality), and a depraved mind (impropriety). So we see that man's heart, soul, and mind have been corrupted by idolatry. The very things that men are supposed to love the Lord his God with he uses for every purpose under the sun except for loving God.

II Timothy 3:13 - "But evil men and impostors will proceed from bad to worse, deceiving and being deceived" (NASB).

In his fallen state man is worthless and useless, he is totally depraved. This is why we read, "All have turned aside, together they have become useless; there is none who does good, there is not even one" (Romans 3:12, NASB). So you see that total depravity means that all of man, his heart, soul, and mind, is corrupted by sin and is not used properly by any man to worship God. The word depraved or reprobate is used to denote that which does not pass the test. It was used to speak of metals that were rejected by refiners because of impurities. The impure metals were discarded and therefore considered useless and worthless. This is the state of all men who have not been regenerated and cleansed and purified through the gospel (Weber, 2014).

The entire Bible is powerful but **Romans** provides a particular depth in understanding the human condition, the tragedy of sin and scope of divine redemption. In seeking to understand and discern the current world situation and the immense falling away from godly standards I have been pondering this portion a lot. It describes the inherent natural tendency to sin in each person's heart since the fall of Adam.

"And just as they did not see fit to acknowledge God any longer, God gave them over to a depraved mind, to do those things which are not proper" (**Romans 1:28, NASB**). Contrast this with those who diligently seek and find it immensely worthwhile to retain the knowledge of God. They study the Scriptures and seek to live by them. They realize the supreme call of the Proverb that cautions its readers, "Watch over your heart with all diligence, For from it flow the springs of life" (**Proverbs 4:23, NASB**). Retaining the knowledge of God is a lifelong pursuit, something we must be committed to.

But many, really most, do "not think it worthwhile to retain the knowledge of God." Instead they have chosen the heavily trampled broad way which leads to destruction

Matthew 7:13-14 - "Enter through the narrow gate; for the gate is wide and the way is broad that leads to destruction, and there are many who enter through it. For the gate is small and the way is narrow that leads to life, and there are few who find it" (**NASB**).

Substitutes for the knowledge of God abound materially, philosophically, educationally, and even in the spiritual realm. These substitutes are billed as "the real thing" and any other outlook may be ridiculed or viewed as "behind the times."

Galatians 6:8 - "For the one who sows to his own flesh will from the flesh reap corruption, but the one who sows to the Spirit will from the Spirit reap eternal life" (**NASB**).

There is a grave consequence in failing to retain the knowledge of God. "God gave them over to a depraved mind." The Precept Austin commentary notes that this depraved mind "speaks of a mind that is so clouded by sin that it is no longer able to make reliable moral judgments. Here we have gone beyond deliberate iniquity to something much more frightening. At this stage people have lost the desire and the ability to think clearly. They have lost their mind and don't even know it. The result is a world that has left God far behind. It is a society with all restraints removed, a culture devoid of all sense of right and wrong, where every one is doing what is 'right in his own eyes'" (Weber, 2014).

Romans 1:28-32 - "And just as they did not see fit to acknowledge God any longer, God gave them over to a depraved mind, to do those things which are not proper, being filled with all unrighteousness, wickedness, greed, evil; full of envy, murder, strife, deceit, malice; *they are* gossips, slanderers, haters of God, insolent, arrogant, boastful, inventors of evil, disobedient to parents, without understanding, untrustworthy, unloving, unmerciful; and although they know the ordinance of God, that those who practice such things are worthy of death, they not only do the same, but also give hearty approval to those who practice them" (**NASB**).

The depraved mind has a predetermined and inevitable disposition to do those things which are not proper, the depraved mind is bent toward impropriety. The depraved mind does not dwell on whatever is honorable, whatever is right, whatever is pure, whatever is lovely, whatever is of good repute, whatever is excellent, or whatever is worthy of praise, instead the depraved mind dwells on the exact opposites. The depraved mind fills itself with all unrighteousness, wickedness, greed, and evil.

Let's look at some of these negative and condemning improprieties that all men everywhere are guilty of in some form or fashion:

Unrighteousness...... that which is not right
Wickedness.............. that which is ungodly, evil, or morally bad

Greed...................... desiring what others have, itching for more, covetous

Evil........................... ill will, malice, malignity, a desire to injure

Envy........................ to feel displeasure and ill will over another's happiness, success, reputation, or possessions. Envy causes hatred toward another because he or she has something that you want or are something that you cannot be, it was for envy that the Jewish leaders delivered over Jesus to Pilate.

Matthew 27:18 - For he knew that because of envy they had handed Him over" (**NASB**)

Murder.................... Murder is just one step beyond envy although there are other reasons that men murder besides envy.

Strife........................ contention or wrangling

Deceit...................... this word in the Greek means "fish-bait" and came to mean to lure, to ensnare, to beguile, to deceive. When a man lies – about anything – he is deceiving. When a man holds back the truth by not speaking it when he should – he is deceiving.

Malice...................... a desire to inflict harm or suffering on another

Gossips.................... secret slanderers, whisperers, tattlers, idle talk about the private affairs of others.

Slanderers................ backbiters using false and defamatory statements or reports in order to injure the character and influence of another.

Haters of God........... hateful to God

Insolent.................... boldly rude or disrespectful; despiteful; insults others

Arrogant....................	proud or haughty; showing oneself above others, with overbearing air of superiority and treating others with contempt
Boastful.....................	the one who speaks with excessive pride especially about himself concerning that which he does not really possess – one may even boast in his humility!
Inventors of evil........	always looking for and finding new ways to sin
Unloving....................	without natural affection
Untrustworthy...........	covenant breakers; without good faith; promise breakers
Unmerciful.................	without mercy, cruel.
Disobedient to parents..............	are you surprised that this is an indication of a depraved mind?
Without understanding.............	without spiritual or moral understanding; spiritual stupidity

(Weber, 2014).

The heathen are under sin and therefore rightly under God's wrath and they are without excuse. There is only one remedy, the gospel! Since God has given man over to depravity and depravity is a judgment of God on sinful man then we cannot legislate or mandate morality but must go with the gospel to sinners for it and it alone is the power of God unto salvation for everyone who believes.

Retaining the knowledge of God is a lifelong pursuit.

CHAPTER 11

THE BLIND MIND

People who are spiritually blind have no vision of what God can do for them or what they can do for God. I pity them. Blindness of the mind is more crippling than physical blindness. Most people who are mentally blind don't know it. We often wonder, "Why can't he see what is happening?" because he really can't see. He is a victim of what psychologists call a faulty "mind set." It means his mind is set in a certain way and cannot be changed. His condition is worse than being physically blind. One reason it's worse is because mental blindness often leads to spiritual blindness. A spiritually blind person can't accept the claims of God because he "just can't see it." this is a great obstacle for the Spirit of God to overcome (Salmon, 2005).

II Corinthians 4:4 - "In whom the god of this world hath blinded the minds of them which believe not, lest the light of the glorious gospel of Christ, who is the image of God, should shine unto them" (**KJV**).

Perhaps you have had conversations with unbelievers that were characteristic of such "blindness." The person with whom you were talking just didn't see it as you attempted to share the truth of Christ. Such responses should not surprise us.

John 9:39 - "And Jesus said, For judgment I am come into this world, that they which see not might see; and that they which see might be made blind" (**KJV**).

Isaiah 35:5 - Then will the eyes of the blind be opened and the ears of the deaf unstopped" (**KJV**).

Psalm 146:8 - "The Lord openeth the eyes of the blind: the Lord raiseth them that are bowed down: the Lord loveth the righteous" (**KJV**).

The blind cannot see even the brightness of the noon-day sun. The eye of the soul has to receive sight first. So, in the mission to the Gentiles given to the Apostle on his conversion, his first work was "to open their eyes, to turn them from darkness to light".

II Corinthians 4:4-6 - "In whom the god of this world hath blinded the minds of them which believe not, lest the light of the glorious gospel of Christ, who is the image of God, should shine unto them. For we preach not ourselves, but Christ Jesus the Lord; and ourselves your servants for Jesus' sake. For God, who commanded the light to shine out of darkness, hath shined in our hearts, to give the light of the knowledge of the glory of God in the face of Jesus Christ" (**KJV**).

Spiritual understanding may be granted only when a true heart turns toward God, when a true heart reaches for God. So for those who are lost we can only introduce the message of salvation through Jesus Christ.

Mark 4:11-12 - "And he said unto them, Unto you it is given to know the mystery of the kingdom of God: but unto them that are without, all these things are done in parables: That seeing they may see, and not perceive; and hearing they may hear, and not understand; lest at any time they should be converted, and their sins should be forgiven them" (**KJV**).

All of a sudden things made more sense. I remember there have been those in my life who would dismiss what I had to say about Faith and

God in a way that was almost offensive. In addition, there were those who were openly offensive suggesting that the entire idea was stupid and fanatical, or a primitive need to explain things we could not. That faith was a concept for the less intelligent who could not or would not grasp the intellectual realities.

Also there were those who would try to use my faith against me to further their political opinions by quoting Bible passages out of context. Or a non believer trying to tell me that I am a hypocrite because I do not agree with them. Further stating my Bible agrees with their position but I do not. Using my faith as a weapon against me in their argument.

I now understand that their opinions have been manipulated by the enemy. The enemy has blinded the mind to the truth as I can see it. This changes my perception of how to respond to them. Perhaps I must be more tolerant and I must respond with compassion and love rather than in anger.

1 John 4:4-6 - "Ye are of God, little children, and have overcome them: because greater is he that is in you, than he that is in the world. They are of the world: therefore speak they of the world, and the world heareth them. We are of God: he that knoweth God heareth us; he that is not of God heareth not us. Hereby know we the spirit of truth, and the spirit of error" (**KJV**).

Put your hands over your eyes and block out all the light. Imagine the feelings as you can not see anything. Not that you are not seeing right now, or not that you are seeing just a little, but that you can not see. There is no way to see because you are blind without any light at all, standing in darkness. In that case you rely on what you have learned up to this point. What you have been able to determine from where ever you have learned it to process the world around you. How have your opinions been formed?

Ultimately you rely on your own experiences. If those experiences are limited to lets say a specific data set, all of your opinions rely only on that data set. But imagine new data is then introduced that is contrary to what you learned in the original data set how would you respond to new information? How would you process that new data? Now consider that God must lead you to understanding. That no matter what is said to you, no matter in what manner it is said to you, if you can not understand it by design, it will sound like nonsense in an understanding shaped by the world, and the enemy. He has blinded the mind.

John 12:40 - "He hath blinded their eyes, and hardened their heart; that they should not see with their eyes, nor understand with their heart, and be converted, and I should heal them" (**KJV**).

The enemy is focused on keeping the unbeliever blinded from Spiritual truths. He has blinded the mind. The enemy wants belief as the world believes. He wants focus on self, forsaking all else. Until God turns his eyes to you, until God lifts the blindness from your spiritual eyes, you can not really see. Not all the explanation in the world will give you spiritual sight. God alone chooses you, to give you spiritual sight. Think about that for a moment. If you are like me and have people you love who you have been talking to, talking and talking to, battling the influence of the world and wondering why there is no response, this is profound. I had an "Ah Ha" moment (Salmon, 2005).

This does not mean that we do not witness as we are called to, it simply means that we introduce the message of salvation through Jesus Christ but only God can save. Wow takes a lot of the pressure off doesn't it? He calls us to make the introduction but we are not tasked with making people come to God. He is chosen and he chooses his flock.

Matthew 28:18-20 - "And Jesus came and spake unto them, saying, All power is given unto me in heaven and in earth. Go ye therefore, and teach all nations, baptizing them in the name of the Father, and of the Son, and of the Holy Ghost: Teaching them to observe all things whatsoever I have commanded you: and, lo, I am with you always, even unto the end of the world. Amen" (**KJV**).

Let's think about that for a moment. He chose us specifically and opened our eyes. He knows who we are and for some reason decided to mold us, shape us into who we have become in service to him. If we are saved he looked at us and reached out to us bringing us to him. We are special, we are loved and we are meant to worship his great name...He shapes our purpose and we walk the path that he is putting before us. No need for fear or worry, only unconditional faith. We belong to him.

We are given the choice when our eyes are opened. Some of us will reject the spirit, for what reasons I can not imagine, but some will. To those we can only feel sorrow. If God has chosen you and chosen to open your eyes to the truth of this world, and the next, how could you reject that? I am perplexed at the notion but we know that some people refuse to be saved even when they have had a glimpse of the truth.

The battleground of the mind is the stronghold. God communicates his word through the mind. The Bible is the written word of God. The enemy fights to keep us veiled from the truth, he wants us to blindly follow our pleasures and desires without thought to ultimate consequence. He has blinded the mind. The enemy wants to stop us from thinking and reasoning keeping us focused on self, our emotion. It is through the mind that the Gospel can break through and offer us reason and purpose beyond self (Salmon, 2005).

When we turn to God and we reach for him God sees us. When God chooses us he opens our mind to the truth through his Gospel. With time he opens our eyes through the Holy Spirit and we become Spiritually aware. A wonderful gift:

Acts 1:8 - "But ye shall receive power, after that the Holy Ghost is come upon you: and ye shall be witnesses unto me both in Jerusalem, and in all Judaea, and in Samaria, and unto the uttermost part of the earth" (**KJV**).

As a true believer we must set an example and we are held to a higher standard. Yes, we can get caught up in things of the world. It is hard to walk in the world and not be affected by it. But we are tasked with keeping our mind and heart in the Spirit.

We are responsible for the introduction through the Great Commission. We must witness, introduce God to the masses. Make the Bible a household word, make the Bible available to all, take a stand against those who would curtail the effectiveness of communication through the mind. Fight to overcome all the obstacles the enemy continues to put in place, all the distractions that are so tempting to remove the mind in favor of the flesh and desire. Make the truth known to all so that they can have the opportunity to be chosen by God. That my friends is our responsibility...

Isaiah 42:16-18 - "And I will bring the blind by a way that they knew not; I will lead them in paths that they have not known: I will make darkness light before them, and crooked things straight. These things will I do unto them, and not forsake them. They shall be turned back, they shall be greatly ashamed, that trust in graven images, that say to the molten images, Ye are our gods. Hear, ye deaf; and look, ye blind, that ye may see" (**KJV**).

We must understand that those who are not yet a believer are fighting an uphill battle to understanding. The enemy has blinded the mind and is trying to make sure that they do not understand so he does not lose them in favor of salvation. So as they resist with their ridiculous arguments do not dismay be patient, be tolerant and be kind. It is our responsibility to share the message but it is God who will save them.

God communicates his word through the mind.

CHAPTER 12

SOBER MINDED

Even though they did not always live by it, the ancients considered "moderation in all things" as the ultimate ideal. When and if this ultimate equilibrium could be reached, life would be most pleasant.

Yet we, as humans, are not always well-balanced creatures. We often go to extremes. In some aspects of life, we may practice self-denial; in others, we throw ourselves into consumption. Our imbalances lead to feelings of craving or guilt (Longhenry, 2009).

We would do well, therefore, to maintain a "sound mind" and to be "sober," or, as in other versions, to exhibit self-control and sober-mindedness. These attributes require discipline and balance, striving to be neither too stringent nor too lax. Several places in the New Testament speak of being sober-minded:

I Peter 4:7 - "But the end of all things is at hand: be ye therefore sober, and watch unto prayer" (**KJV**).

I Peter 5:8 - "Be sober, be vigilant; because your adversary the devil, as a roaring lion, walketh about, seeking whom he may devour" (**KJV**).

Titus 2:2 - "That the aged men be sober, grave, temperate, sound in faith, in charity, in patience" (**KJV**).

Titus 2:6 - "Young men likewise exhort to be sober minded" (**KJV**).

I Corinthians 15:34 - "Awake to righteousness, and sin not; for some have not the knowledge of God: I speak this to your shame" (**KJV**).

II Timothy 4:5 - "But watch thou in all things, endure afflictions, do the work of an evangelist, make full proof of thy ministry" (**KJV**).

Paul exhorts Timothy to be "sober-minded, endure suffering, do the work of an evangelist, fulfill your ministry". The term *sober-minded* literally means "free from intoxicating influences." We speak of a person who is not drunk with alcohol or high on drugs as being "sober." His or her mind is not under the control of a dangerous outside force (Longhenry, 2009).

More broadly, being sober-minded means that we do not allow ourselves to be captivated by any type of influence that would lead us away from sound judgment. The sober-minded individual is not "intoxicated," figuratively speaking, and is therefore calm under pressure, self-controlled in all areas, and rational.

One of the qualifications for an elder or church leader is that they and their wives be sober-minded

I Timothy 3:2 - "A bishop then must be blameless, the husband of one wife, vigilant, sober, of good behaviour, given to hospitality, apt to teach" (**KJV**).

I Timothy 3:11 - "Even so must their wives be grave, not slanderers, sober, faithful in all things" (**KJV**).

Titus 1:8 - "But a lover of hospitality, a lover of good men, sober, just, holy, temperate" (**KJV**).

That is, they should live in reverential awe of their responsibility as representatives of Christ

II Corinthians 5:20 - "Now then we are ambassadors for Christ, as though God did beseech you by us: we pray you in Christ's stead, be ye reconciled to God" (**KJV**).

Peter warned that "the end of all things is at hand; therefore be self-controlled and sober-minded for the sake of your prayers"

I Peter 4:7 - "But the end of all things is at hand: be ye therefore sober, and watch unto prayer" (**KJV**).

Those who are sober-minded will be alert to the need to pray and take the occasion to pray at opportune times.

More often than not, we see the opposite of sober-mindedness displayed in our world. Silliness, irresponsible choices, foolish experimentation with harmful substances or behaviors, and crude joking are in direct opposition to the command to be sober-minded.

Ephesians 5:3-4 - "But fornication, and all uncleanness, or covetousness, let it not be once named among you, as becometh saints; Neither filthiness, nor foolish talking, nor jesting, which are not convenient: but rather giving of thanks" (**KJV**).

The passage lists some behaviors that conflict with sober-minded living: "But among you there must not be even a hint of sexual immorality, or of any kind of impurity, or of greed, because these are improper for God's holy people. Nor should there be obscenity, foolish talk or coarse joking, which are out of place." Then, in case someone should think this is a list of judgmental preferences, Paul goes on to write the following: "For of this you can be sure: No immoral, impure or greedy person, such a person is an idolater, has any inheritance in the kingdom of Christ and of God. Let no one deceive you with empty words, for because of such things God's wrath comes on those who are disobedient (Longhenry, 2009). Therefore do not be partners with them:

Ephesians 5:5-7 - "For this ye know, that no whoremonger, nor unclean person, nor covetous man, who is an idolater, hath any inheritance in the kingdom of Christ and of God. Let no man deceive you with vain words: for because of these things cometh the wrath of God upon the children of disobedience. Be not ye therefore partakers with them" (**KJV**).

Being sober-minded does not mean living a sour, joyless existence. In fact, sober-minded Christians are to be continually filled with the joy of the Holy Spirit

Galatians 5:22 - "But the fruit of the Spirit is love, joy, peace, longsuffering, gentleness, goodness, faith" (**KJV**).

Acts 15:32 - "And Judas and Silas, being prophets also themselves, exhorted the brethren with many words, and confirmed them" (**KJV**).

Romans 14:17 - "For the kingdom of God is not meat and drink; but righteousness, and peace, and joy in the Holy Ghost" (**KJV**).

Eliminating foolishness, frivolity, and mind-numbing silliness from our lives allows us to focus on what is real, eternal, and inspiring. Jesus' command to His sleepy-headed disciples suggests the need for sober-mindedness: "Watch and pray so that you will not fall into temptation" Rather, clothe yourselves with the Lord Jesus Christ, and do not think about how to gratify the desires of the flesh." And that is a good description of being sober-minded. In:

Romans 13:12-14 - "The night is far spent, the day is at hand: let us therefore cast off the works of darkness, and let us put on the armour of light. Let us walk honestly, as in the day; not in rioting and drunkenness, not in chambering and wantonness, not in strife and envying. But put ye on the Lord Jesus Christ, and make not provision for the flesh, to fulfill the lusts thereof" (**KJV**).

Paul explains the urgency behind the frequent commands to be sober-minded: "The night is nearly over; the day is almost here. So let us put aside the deeds of darkness and put on the armor of light. Let us behave decently, as in the daytime, not in carousing and drunkenness, not in sexual immorality and debauchery, not in dissension and jealousy.

After teaching the great doctrine regarding the gospel of God's righteousness that is ours through faith in Christ in **Romans chapters 1-11**, Paul begins to exhort us to godly living. How are we to live in light of the saving power of the gospel? That is what **Romans 12-16** aims to teach. The practical section of Romans begins with a great "therefore." Seeing all that God did on our behalf, therefore live like this. The first of Paul's great exhortations is to be renewed in our minds: "I appeal to you therefore, brothers, by the mercies of God, to present your bodies as a living sacrifice, holy and acceptable to God, which is your spiritual worship.

Do not be conformed to this world, but be transformed by the renewal of your mind, that by testing you may discern what is the will of God, what is good and acceptable and perfect". The phrase "transformed by the renewing of the mind" is found in:

Romans 12:2 - "And be not conformed to this world: but be ye transformed by the renewing of your mind, that ye may prove what is that good, and acceptable, and perfect, will of God" (**KJV**).

Chapter 12 marks the transition in that epistle from the apostle Paul's theological teaching to his practical teaching. The **Book of Romans** is probably the closest thing in the Bible to a systematic theology. Paul did not found the church at Rome, but he had every intention of visiting that church on his way to Spain. As a result, Paul wrote this epistle as a way of introducing himself to that congregation and to give them an overview of the gospel and

Mark 14:38 - "Watch ye and pray, lest ye enter into temptation. The spirit truly is ready, but the flesh is weak" **(KJV)**.

Ephesians 5:18 - "And be not drunk with wine, wherein is excess; but be filled with the Spirit" **(KJV)**.

Paul commands us to avoid being filled with wine, because that leads to debauchery, but rather to be continually filled with the Holy Spirit. This verse implies that we can only be one of those, but not both. It's an either/or proposition. If we pursue drunkenness, we cannot also pursue God. If substances control us, we cannot also be controlled by the Holy Spirit. Sober-minded people choose to abstain from practices that would lead them into sin.

Romans 12:1-2 - "I beseech you therefore, brethren, by the mercies of God, that ye present your bodies a living sacrifice, holy, acceptable unto God, which is your reasonable service. And be not conformed to this world: but be ye transformed by the renewing of your mind, that ye may prove what is that good, and acceptable, and perfect, will of God" **(KJV)**.

The phrase "the mercies of God" refers to all of what has preceded in **Romans chapters 1-11**. The exhortation that Paul presents is that since we have been the gracious recipients of God's great mercies, we are to be "living sacrifices" to God. How do we do this? We are living sacrifices to God by not conforming to this world, but by being transformed by the renewal of our minds.

This exhortation really serves as a summary statement of all that follows. A living sacrifice to God is one who does not conform, but is transformed. We are not to be conformed to this world. Paul is using the word *world* here to refer to the spirit of the age. In other words, *world* refers to the popular worldview that rejects God and His revelation. As unbelievers, we are naturally conformed to the world

Ephesians 2:1-3 - "And you hath he quickened, who were dead in trespasses and sins; Wherein in time past ye walked according to the course of this world, according to the prince of the power of the air, the spirit that now worketh in the children of disobedience: Among whom also we all had our conversation in times past in the lusts of our flesh, fulfilling the desires of the flesh and of the mind; and were by nature the children of wrath, even as others" (**KJV**).

As believers, we are no longer conformed to this world because we no longer belong to the spirit of this age. We have been translated from the kingdom of darkness into the kingdom of God's beloved Son:

Colossians 1:13 - "Who hath delivered us from the power of darkness, and hath translated us into the kingdom of his dear Son" (**KJV**).

Therefore, rather than continuing to conform to this world, we are to be transformed by having our minds renewed.

It is interesting to note that Paul says that we must be transformed by the renewing of our "minds." The mind is the key to the Christian life. The reason why non-Christians do not respond to Christian truth is that they cannot discern spiritual truth

I Corinthians 2:14 - "But the natural man receiveth not the things of the Spirit of God: for they are foolishness unto him: neither can he know them, because they are spiritually discerned" (**KJV**).

The gospel is a call for the unbeliever to repent of his sin and embrace Christ by faith. The Greek word translated "repentance" carries the notion of a change of mind. Our thinking must be changed (transformed) from old, ungodly ways of thinking into new, godly ways of thinking. What we know in our minds to be true forms a conviction in our hearts of that truth, and that conviction in our hearts translates into action. Therefore, we must first renew our minds.

Thinking is to replace it with God's truth, and the only infallible source of God's truth is His revealed Word, the Bible. Transformation through renewed minds comes as believers expose themselves to God's Word through the faithful exposition of it each week in church, personal Bible study, and group Bible study. A solid church that believes in preaching the Word, reading the Word, and singing the Word is invaluable in helping us renew our minds.

There are no shortcuts. There is no magical formula for renewing our minds. We must fill our minds with God's Word. As Jesus prayed to the Father:

John 17:17 - "Sanctify them through thy truth: thy word is truth" (**KJV**).

In this circumstance, would knowing that Jesus is returning tomorrow change the way you lived? Would it lead you to "straighten up" and apply yourself more diligently to self-control and sober-mindedness? Even though we may not know for certain whether Jesus will come today, tomorrow, or in a thousand years, the New Testament makes clear that we must live as if He will return momentarily. Let us develop self-control and sober-mindedness so that we may be found faithful in the Kingdom!

We must fill our minds with God's Word.

CHAPTER 13

ONE MIND OR SAME MIND

If a number of people are **of one mind, of like mind**, or **of the same mind**, they all agree about something.

Romans 12:15-16 - "Rejoice with those who rejoice, and weep with those who weep. Be of the same mind toward one another; do not be haughty in mind, but associate with the lowly. Do not be wise in your own estimation" (**NASB**).

Romans 15:5 - "Now may the God who gives perseverance and encouragement grant you to be of the same mind with one another according to Christ Jesus" (**NASB**).

I Peter 3:8 - "To sum up, all of you be harmonious, sympathetic, brotherly, kindhearted, and humble in spirit" (**NASB**).

Here three verses are unanimous in telling us to be of the same mind one toward another. The thought is to try to put self in the other person's place and to think the other person's thoughts. **Romans 12:16** is closely linked with the preceding **verse 15**, "Rejoice with those who rejoice, and weep with those who weep." Some translate the expression "Be of the same mind," as "Have full sympathy with." Others make it, "same respect one for another." The word means "concord" or "unanimity"; whether it be opinion or feeling, depends on the context. Here it probably refers to feeling, while in **Romans 15:5**, it would seem to be of opinion.

The mind of Christ: Some may say, "How can we be of one mind? There is such a variety among Christians; so many different opinions, it seems impossible to agree on everything." Here are two considerations in connection with this problem. First, let each Christian be desirous of obtaining the mind of Christ in every matter. With earnest prayer and supplication, the will of our Lord will be revealed through His precious Word. Second, the Word of God should be searched to see if there is any Scripture definitely dealing with the subject under question. If there is such a Scripture, then each one must be willing to submit to it as an order from our Lord and Master. If Christ is the touchstone of our faith, and it is our desire to please Him and walk in His ways, we will get along. If we make Christ our center, and purpose in our hearts to make His will foremost in our lives, we will not quarrel among ourselves and do things unworthy of His precious name.

The ambitious guests in Luke:

Luke 14:7-11 - "And He *began* speaking a parable to the invited guests when He noticed how they had been picking out the places of honor *at the table*, saying to them, "When you are invited by someone to a wedding feast, do not [a]take the place of honor, for someone more distinguished than you may have been invited by him, and he who invited you both will come and say to you, 'Give *your* place to this man,' and then in disgrace you proceed to occupy the last place. But when you are invited, go and recline at the last place, so that when the one who has invited you comes, he may say to you, 'Friend, move up higher'; then you will have honor in the sight of all who are at the table with you. For everyone who exalts himself will be humbled, and he who humbles himself will be exalted" (**NASB**).

We have the story of the ambitious guests. The Lord had been invited to a dinner in a Pharisee's house, along with others. He noticed that many of them tried to get into the most honored seats. He says in **verses 8-10**, "When you are invited by anyone to a wedding feast, do not sit down in the best place, lest one more honorable than you be invited by him; and he who invited you and him come and say to you, 'Give place to this man,' and then you begin with shame to take the lowest place. But when you are invited, go and sit down in the lowest place, so that when he who invited you comes he may say to you, 'Friend, go up higher.' Then you will have glory in the presence of those who sit at the table with you."

In a world where there is so much to divide us, how do we remain united as Christians? Paul provides direction on being of one mind in his letter to the Philippians.

Philippians 2:1-4 - "Therefore if there is any encouragement in Christ, if there is any consolation of love, if there is any fellowship of the Spirit, if any affection and compassion, make my joy complete by being of the same mind, maintaining the same love, united in spirit, intent on one purpose. Do nothing from selfishness or empty conceit, but with humility of mind regard one another as more important than yourselves; do not *merely* look out for your own personal interests, but also for the interests of others" (**NASB**).

Paul knew that these saints at Philippi loved him. They had sent once and again to relieve his necessities, so he pleaded with them, by their love to him, to love each other. He does as much as say, "If you really do love me, if it is not a sham, if you have any sympathy with me, and with my labours and sufferings, if you really have the same spirit that burns in my breast, make my heart full of joy by clinging to one another, by being like-minded, 'having the same love, being of one accord, of one mind.'"

In Romans Paul says:

Romans 15:6 - "That ye may with one mind and one mouth glorify God, even the Father of our Lord Jesus Christ" (**KJV**).

Romans 12:16 - "Be of the same mind one toward another. Mind not high things, but condescend to men of low estate. Be not wise in your own conceits" (**KJV**).

Having the mind of Christ means we "look at life from our Savior's point of view, having His values and desires in mind. It means to think God's thoughts and not think as the world thinks." It is a shared perspective of humility, compassion, and dependence on God.

Philippians 2:5-11 - "Let this mind be in you, which was also in Christ Jesus: Who, being in the form of God, thought it not robbery to be equal with God: But made himself of no reputation, and took upon him the form of a servant, and was made in the likeness of men: And being found in fashion as a man, he humbled himself, and became obedient unto death, even the death of the cross. Wherefore God also hath highly exalted him, and given him a name which is above every name: That at the name of Jesus every knee should bow, of things in heaven, and things in earth, and things under the earth; And that every tongue should confess that Jesus Christ is Lord, to the glory of God the Father" (**KJV**).

Walking in unity does not mean that we always have the same ideas about the same issues. We may have differences of opinion from time to time. That is both healthy and good. But being of one mind in Christ means that I will humble myself, even if no one else seems to be making any attempt at humility. In sum, being of one mind means humbling myself just as Christ our God humbled Himself.

Romans 8:9 says, "However, you are not in the flesh but in the Spirit, if indeed the Spirit of God dwells in you. But if anyone does not have the Spirit of Christ, he does not belong to Him" (**NASB**).

After salvation, a believer's responsibility is to yield to the Holy Spirit's leading and let the Spirit transform his life.

Our unity is in Jesus Christ. It is God's power in the cross of Jesus Christ that has formed us into a community. We are one in Christ through faith; we are one with each other since we have One Lord, One Faith, One Baptism. If we come together in one mind and one purpose, then we live out what we already are, Christ's Church, and then we become truly the people God wants us to be. As we accept each other, speak well of each other, interpret the actions of each other in the kindest way, love each other, we come closer to Christ. As we learn and study and pray, we come closer to the cross of Christ and to each other. Amen.

One Mind or Same Mind

CHAPTER 14

WILLING MIND

David told Solomon to be careful to obey every one of God's commands to ensure Israel's prosperity and the continuation of David's descendants upon the throne. It was the king's solemn duty to study and obey god's laws. The teachings of Scripture are the keys to security, happiness, and justice, but y9ou'll never discover them unless you search God's Word. If we ignore God's will and neglect his teaching, anything we attempt to build, even if it has God's name on it, will be headed for collapse. Get to know God's commands through regular Bible study, and find ways to apply them consistently.

I Chronicles 28:9 - "And Solomon, my son, learn to know the God of your ancestors intimately. Worship and serve him with your whole heart and a willing mind. For the Lord sees every heart and knows every plan and thought. If you seek him, you will find him. But if you forsake him, he will reject you forever" (**NLT**).

We need to have a willing mind. A mind which is willing to submit to God and His commands. A willing mind is one the freely surrenders to God and His will. It is the type of mind that will read God's word and obey it's instructions. A mind that freely states, "Yes Lord I will do that!"

Now we all know that having a willing mind is not always easy. In fact most of us do not have a willing mind most of the time. Most of us are more like Jonah when God told him; "Arise, go to Nineveh, that great city, and cry out against it; for their wickedness has come up before Me. But Jonah arose to flee to Tarshish from the presence of the LORD." No willing mind there.

We need to more like Isaiah, "also I heard the voice of the Lord, saying: "Whom shall I send, And who will go for Us?" Then I said, "Here am I! Send me." He certainly had a willing mind. We all need to have willing minds. Minds willing to obey God's call, His commands, His will. We also need to have a ready mind.

II Corinthians 8:19 - "And not that only, but who was also chosen of the churches to travel with us with this grace, which is administered by us to the glory of the same Lord, and declaration of your ready mind" (**KJV**).

We need not only be willing but ready. We need to ready to respond to the call of the Lord.

In **Titus 3:1** - "Remind the people to be subject to rulers and authorities, to be obedient, to be ready to do whatever is good" (**NIV**).

We are told; "Remind them to be subject to rulers and authorities, to obey, to be ready for every good work". Paul tell us in the book of **Romans:**

Romans 1:15 - "That is why I am so eager to preach the gospel also to you who are in Rome" (**NIV**).

Let me ask you are you ready for "every good work". Ready to serve others, ready to put other first. Are you ready to serve the church any way you can? Are you ready to preach the gospel? To share the good news of Jesus Christ to those whom God places in you path?

Do you have a ready mind?

CHAPTER 15

RENEWAL OF THE MIND

The only possible way to avoid being conformed into the image of this world is to be transformed by the renewing or renewal of the mind. Again, there is no transformation possible until the Spirit of God quickens someone to new life because dead men can't raise themselves.

Ephesians 2:1 - "And you he made alive, when you were dead through the trespasses and sins" (**RSV**).

Ephesians 2:5 - "Even when we were dead through our trespasses, made us alive together with Christ (by grace you have been saved)" (**RSV**).

We must become new creations in Jesus Christ before we can even hope to transform ourselves into the image of Christ. The Christian alternative to immoral behaviors is not a new list of moral behaviors. It is the triumphant power and transformation of the Holy Spirit through faith in Jesus Christ, our Savior, our Lord, and our Treasure.

II Corinthians 6:17 - "Therefore come out from them, and be separate from them, says the Lord, and touch nothing unclean; then I will welcome you" (**RSV**).

The phrase "transformed by the renewing of the mind" is found in:

Romans 12:2 - "Do not be conformed to this world but be transformed by the renewal of your mind, that you may prove what is the will of God, what is good and acceptable and perfect" (**RSV**).

Renewing your mind should not be confused with thoughts that come into your mind. Many times we cannot stop certain thoughts from entering our mind. But what we do with that thought the instant we recognize that thought-that's where our response clearly shows whether or not we are renewing our mind. **Chapter 12** marks the transition in that epistle from the apostle Paul's theological teaching to his practical teaching. The Book of Romans is probably the closest thing in the Bible to a systematic theology. Paul did not found the church at Rome, but he had every intention of visiting that church on his way to Spain. As a result, Paul wrote this epistle as a way of introducing himself to that congregation and to give them an overview of the gospel and what it means in the lives of believers.

After teaching the great doctrine regarding the gospel of God's righteousness that is ours through faith in Christ in Romans chapters 1-11, Paul begins to exhort us to godly living. How are we to live in light of the saving power of the gospel? That is what Romans chapters 12-16 aims to teach. The practical section of Romans begins with a great "therefore." Seeing all that God did on our behalf, therefore live like this. The first of Paul's great exhortations is to be renewed in our minds:

Romans 12:1-2 - "I appeal to you therefore, brethren, by the mercies of God, to present your bodies as a living sacrifice, holy and acceptable to God, which is your spiritual worship. Do not be conformed to this world but be transformed by the renewal of your mind, that you may prove what is the will of God, what is good and acceptable and perfect" (**RSV**).

The exhortation that Paul presents is that since we have been the gracious recipients of God's great mercies, we are to be "living sacrifices" to God. How do we do this? We are living sacrifices to God by not conforming to this world, but by being transformed by the renewal of our minds.

This exhortation really serves as a summary statement of all that follows. A living sacrifice to God is one who does not conform, but is transformed. We are not to be conformed to this world. Paul is using the word world here to refer to the spirit of the age. In other words, world refers to the popular worldview that rejects God and His revelation. As unbelievers, we are naturally conformed to the world

Ephesians 2:1-3 - "And you he made alive, when you were dead through the trespasses and sins in which you once walked, following the course of this world, following the prince of the power of the air, the spirit that is now at work in the sons of disobedience. Among these we all once lived in the passions of our flesh, following the desires of body and mind, and so we were by nature children of wrath, like the rest of mankind" (**RSV**).

As believers, we are no longer conformed to this world because we no longer belong to the spirit of this age. We have been translated from the kingdom of darkness into the kingdom of God's beloved Son. Renewing your mind is a process, not a one time achievement.

Colossians 1:13 - "He has delivered us from the dominion of darkness and transferred us to the kingdom of his beloved Son" (**RSV**).

Therefore, rather than continuing to conform to this world, we are to be transformed by having our minds renewed.

It is interesting to note that Paul says that we must be transformed by the renewing of our "minds." The mind is the key to the Christian life. The reason why non-Christians do not respond to Christian truth is that they cannot discern spiritual truth

I Corinthians 2:14 - "The unspiritual man does not receive the gifts of the Spirit of God, for they are folly to him, and he is not able to understand them because they are spiritually discerned" (**RSV**).

The gospel is a call for the unbeliever to repent of his sin and embrace Christ by faith. The Greek word translated "repentance" carries the notion of a change of mind. Our thinking must be changed (transformed) from old, ungodly ways of thinking into new, godly ways of thinking. What we know in our minds to be true forms a conviction in our hearts of that truth, and that conviction in our hearts translates into action. Therefore, we must first renew our minds.

The only way to replace the error of the world's way of thinking is to replace it with God's truth, and the only infallible source of God's truth is His revealed Word, the Bible. Transformation through renewed minds comes as believers expose themselves to God's Word through the faithful exposition of it each week in church, personal Bible study, and group Bible study. A solid church that believes in preaching the Word, reading the Word, and singing the Word is invaluable in helping us renew our minds.

There are no shortcuts. There is no magical formula for renewing our minds. We must fill our minds with God's Word. As Jesus prayed to the Father, "Sanctify them in the truth; your word is truth"

John 17:17 - "Sanctify them in the truth; thy word is truth" (**RSV**).

The renewing of the mind brings your will into agreement with the Father's will. As you fill your mind with His Word by reading, thinking about, memorizing, praying, speaking out loud, even singing, you begin to think in a way that pleases Him, and His ways become your ways. You become, through His power and wisdom, a master of the circumstances of life. When difficulties or decisions arise, you automatically view them through the eyes of God's Word. That new perspective changes everything.

The call to Christian maturity is to discipline your thoughts and your emotions Our minds are to be conformed to the mind of Christ. That conformity does not automatically or instantly occur with conversion. Our conversion by the power of the Holy Spirit is not the end of our learning process but the beginning. At conversion we enroll in the school of Christ. There is no graduation this side of heaven. It is a pilgrimage of lifelong education.

The RENEWED mind is the key to the Christian life.

CHAPTER 16

PEACE OF MIND

Most people would define peace of mind as the absence of mental stress and anxiety. The expression "peace of mind" conjures up images of Buddha-like composure wherein calm, comfort, and composure are so prevalent that nothing can disturb the one who has peace of mind. An imperturbable, placid person is said to have peace of mind.

II Corinthians 2:13 - "But I had no peace of mind because my dear brother Titus hadn't yet arrived with a report from you. So I said good-bye and went on to Macedonia to find him" (**NLT**).

Paul says he found no "peace of mind" because he didn't find Titus in Troas. The literal translation of this phrase is "rest of my spirit."

The Bible uses the word *peace* in several different ways. *Peace* sometimes refers to a state of friendship between God and man. This peace between a holy God and sinful mankind has been effected by Christ's sacrificial death, "having made peace through the blood of his cross"

Colossians 1:20 - "And through him God reconciled everything to himself. He made peace with everything in heaven and on earth by means of Christ's blood on the cross" (**NLT**).

In addition, as High Priest the Lord Jesus maintains that state of friendship on behalf of all who continue to "come to God by him, seeing he always lives to make intercession for them".

Hebrews 7:25 - "Therefore he is able, once and forever, to save those who come to God through him. He lives forever to intercede with God on their behalf" (**NLT**).

This state of friendship with God is a prerequisite for the second kind of peace, that which sometimes refers to a tranquil mind. It is only when "we have peace with God through our Lord Jesus Christ"

Romans 5:1 - "Therefore, since we have been made right in God's sight by faith, we have peace with God because of what Jesus Christ our Lord has done for us" (**NLT**).

We can experience the true peace of mind that is a fruit of the Holy Spirit, in other words, His fruit exhibited in us.

Galatians 5:22 - "But the Holy Spirit produces this kind of fruit in our lives: love, joy, peace, patience, kindness, goodness, faithfulness" (**NLT**).

Isaiah 26:3 - "You will keep in perfect peace all who trust in you, all whose thoughts are fixed on you" (**NLT**)!

This passage tells us that God will keep us in "perfect peace" if our minds are "stayed" on Him, meaning our minds lean on Him, center on Him, and trust in Him. Our tranquility of mind is "perfect" or imperfect to the degree that the "mind is stayed on" God rather than ourselves or on our problems. Peace is experienced as we believe what the Bible says about God's nearness as in:

Psalm 139:1-12 - "O LORD, you have examined my heart and know everything about me. You know when I sit down or stand up. You know my thoughts even when I'm far away. You see me when I travel and when

I rest at home. You know everything I do. You know what I am going to say even before I say it, LORD. You go before me and follow me. You place your hand of blessing on my head. Such knowledge is too wonderful for me, too great for me to understand I can never escape from your Spirit! I can never get away from your presence! If I go up to heaven, you are there; if I go down to the grave, you are there. If I ride the wings of the morning, if I dwell by the farthest oceans, even there your hand will guide me, and your strength will support me. I could ask the darkness to hide me and the light around me to become night, but even in darkness I cannot hide from you. To you the night shines as bright as day. Darkness and light are the same to you" (**NLT**).

This passage speaks about His goodness and power, His mercy and love for His children, and His complete sovereignty over all of life's circumstances. But we can't trust someone we don't know, and it is crucial, therefore, to come to know intimately the Prince of Peace, Jesus Christ. Peace is experienced as a result of prayer. "Be anxious for nothing, but in everything by prayer and supplication, with thanksgiving, let your requests be made known to God; and the peace of God which surpasses all understanding, will guard your hearts and minds through Christ Jesus".

Philippians 4:6-7 - "Don't worry about anything; instead, pray about everything. Tell God what you need, and thank him for all he has done. Then you will experience God's peace, which exceeds anything we can understand. His peace will guard your hearts and minds as you live in Christ Jesus" (**NLT**).

A peaceful mind and heart are experienced as a result of recognizing that an all-wise and loving Father has a purpose in our trials. "We know that all things work together for good to those who love God and are called according to His purpose."

Romans 8:28 - "And we know that God causes everything to work together for the good of those who love God and are called according to his purpose for them" (**NLT**).

God can bring a variety of good things, including peace, from the afflictions that we experience. Even the discipline and chastening of the Lord will "yield the peaceable fruit of righteousness" in our lives.

Hebrews 12:11 - "No discipline is enjoyable while it is happening, it's painful! But afterward there will be a peaceful harvest of right living for those who are trained in this way" (**NLT**).

They provide a fresh opportunity for "hoping in God" and eventually "praising Him".

Psalm 43:5 - "Why am I discouraged? Why is my heart so sad? I will put my hope in God! I will praise him again, my Savior and my God" (**NLT**)!

They help us "comfort" others when they undergo similar trials

II Corinthians 1:4 - "He comforts us in all our troubles so that we can comfort others. When they are troubled, we will be able to give them the same comfort God has given us" (**NLT**).

And they "achieve for us an eternal glory that far outweighs them all".

II Corinthians 4:17 - "For our present troubles are small and won't last very long. Yet they produce for us a glory that vastly outweighs them and will last forever" (**NLT**)!

Philippians 4:19 - "And this same God who takes care of me will supply all your needs from his glorious riches, which have been given to us in Christ Jesus" (**NLT**).

Peace of mind and the tranquility of spirit that accompanies it are only available when we have true peace with God through the sacrifice of Christ on the cross in payment of our sins. Those who attempt to find peace in worldly pursuits will find themselves sadly deceived. For Christians, however, peace of mind is available through the intimate knowledge of, and complete trust in, the God who meets "all your needs according to his glorious riches in Christ Jesus".

Peace is experienced as a result of prayer.

CHAPTER 17

MIND OF CHRIST

The mind of Christ is something all believers have, as the Apostle Paul said, when speaking to the Christians in Corinth, "we have the mind of Christ". Those who have the mind of Christ are able to discern spiritual things that the natural man (or the unbeliever) cannot understand or see. Having the mind of Christ is the same as being indwelt by the Holy Spirit, and both are attained through faith at the moment of salvation (Roe, 2013).

I Corinthians 2:16 - "For, "Who has known the mind of the Lord so as to instruct him? But we have the mind of Christ" (**NIV**).

Paul quotes and then makes a statement concerning all believers: "We have the mind of Christ." Having the mind of Christ means sharing the plan, purpose, and perspective of Christ, and it is something that all believers possess.

Having the mind of Christ means we understand God's plan in the world, to bring glory to Himself, restore creation to its original splendor, and provide salvation for sinners. It means we identify with Christ's purpose "to seek and to save what was lost".

Luke 19:10 - "For the Son of Man came to seek and to save the lost" (**NIV**).

It means we share Jesus' perspective of humility and obedience:

Philippians 2:5-8 - "In your relationships with one another, have the same mindset as Christ Jesus: Who, being in very nature God, did not consider equality with God something to be used to his own advantage; rather, he made himself nothing by taking the very nature of a servant, being made in human likeness. And being found in appearance as a man, he humbled himself by becoming obedient to death even death on a cross" (**NIV**)!

Compassion:

Matthew 9:36 - "When he saw the crowds, he had compassion on them, because they were harassed and helpless, like sheep without a shepherd" (**NIV**).

And prayerful dependence on God:

Luke 5:16 - "But Jesus often withdrew to lonely places and prayed" (**NIV**).

I Corinthians 2:6-16 - "We do, however, speak a message of wisdom among the mature, but not the wisdom of this age or of the rulers of this age, who are coming to nothing. 7 No, we declare God's wisdom, a mystery that has been hidden and that God destined for our glory before time began. 8 None of the rulers of this age understood it, for if they had, they would not have crucified the Lord of glory. 9 However, as it is written: "What no eye has seen, what no ear has heard, and what no human mind has conceived"—the things God has prepared for those who love him—these are the things God has revealed to us by his Spirit. The Spirit searches all things, even the deep things of God. 11 For who knows a person's thoughts except their own spirit within them? In the same way no one knows the thoughts of God except the Spirit of God. 12 What we have received is not the spirit of the world, but the Spirit who is from God, so that we may understand what God has freely given us. 13 This is what we speak, not in words taught us by human wisdom but in words taught by the Spirit, explaining spiritual realities with Spirit-taught words. 14

The person without the Spirit does not accept the things that come from the Spirit of God but considers them foolishness, and cannot understand them because they are discerned only through the Spirit. 15 The person with the Spirit makes judgments about all things, but such a person is not subject to merely human judgments, 16 for, "Who has known the mind of the Lord so as to instruct him?" But we have the mind of Christ" (**NIV**).

We note some truths concerning the mind of Christ:

1) The mind of Christ stands in sharp contrast to the wisdom of man (**verses 5-6**).
2) The mind of Christ involves wisdom from God, once hidden but now revealed (**verse 7**).
3) The mind of Christ is given to believers through the Spirit of God (**verses 10-12**).
4) The mind of Christ cannot be understood by those without the Spirit (**verse 14**).
5) The mind of Christ gives believers discernment in spiritual matters (**verse 15**). (Roe, 2013).

In order to have the mind of Christ, you must first have saving faith in Christ.

John 1:12 - "Yet to all who did receive him, to those who believed in his name, he gave the right to become children of God" (**NIV**).

I John 5:12 - "Whoever has the Son has life; whoever does not have the Son of God does not have life" (**NIV**).

After salvation, the believer lives a life under God's influence. The Holy Spirit indwells and enlightens the believer, infusing him with wisdom, the mind of Christ. The believer bears a responsibility to yield to the Spirit's leading.

Ephesians 4:30 - "And do not grieve the Holy Spirit of God, with whom you were sealed for the day of redemption" (**NIV**).

And to allow the Spirit to transform and renew our mind:

Romans 12:1-2 - "Therefore, I urge you, brothers and sisters, in view of God's mercy, to offer your bodies as a living sacrifice, holy and pleasing to God—this is your true and proper worship. 2 Do not conform to the pattern of this world, but be transformed by the renewing of your mind. Then you will be able to test and approve what God's will is—his good, pleasing and perfect will" (**NIV**).

Our minds need to be consistently renewed, moving away from the mind of theflesh and into the mind of Christ. Ultimately, all who have the mind of Christ, those who belong to God, will be sanctified, or changed by the new program that has been installed by the Holy Spirit. The process unfolds over a lifetime and God is faithful to bring it to completion.

Having the mind of Christ means sharing the plan, purpose, and perspective of Christ.

REFERENCES

Blaz, Kos, *Your mind is like a garden that needs a good daily care*, Personal Development Psychology, March 20, 2017.

Editor, *God's Thinking vs Man's Thinking*. The Bible Study, WordPress, July 19, 2019.

Ellis, Nanice, Negative Thinking, Wake Up World, August 19, 2015.

Ganz, Richard L., *Ways to Take Your Thoughts Captive*, Crosswalk, December 10, 2000.

Goldstein, Michele, *How to Control Your Thoughts*, Lifeback, July 19, 2018.

GotQuestions, *What does it mean to have a reprobate mind?*, GotQuestions. org., 2014.

Henriques, Gregg, *What is the Mind?* Psychology Today, December 22, 2011.

Longhenry, Ethan, *"Sober Minded"*, DeWard Publishing, March 12. 2009.

Roe, Julie, *Mind of Christ*, Charisma, Charisma Media, March 04, 2013.

Salmon, Charles, *The Blind Mind*, Outreach, Inc., *January 2, 2005*.

Smith, Ed and Joshua, *Double Mindedness*, Transformation Prayer Ministry, August 26, 2016.

The Holy Bible, *King James Version*, (KJV), New York: American Bible Society, 1999.

The Holy Bible, *New American Standard Bible*, (NASB), La Habra, CA: Foundation Publications, for the Lockman Foundation, 1971.

The Holy Bible, *New International Version*, (NIV), Grand Rapids: Zondervan Publishing House, 1984.

The Holy Bible, *New Living Translation*, (NLT), Tyndale House Foundation, 2015.

The Holy Bible, *Revised Standard Version Bible*, (RSV), Division of Christian Education of the National Council of the Churches of Christ in the United States of America, 1989

Weber, Stephen C., *"A Depraved Mind"*, Daily Encouragement, Wordpress, March 10, 2014.

APPENDIX

MIND OF CHRIST

Most Relevant Verses

John 14:9-11

Jesus said to him, "Have I been so long with you, and yet you have not come to know Me, Philip? He who has seen Me has seen the Father; how can you say, 'Show us the Father'? "Do you not believe that I am in the Father, and the Father is in Me? The words that I say to you I do not speak on My own initiative, but the Father abiding in Me does His works. "Believe Me that I am in the Father and the Father is in Me; otherwise believe because of the works themselves.

Matthew 5:17

Do not think that I came to abolish the Law or the Prophets; I did not come to abolish but to fulfill.

John 15:10

If you keep My commandments, you will abide in My love; just as I have kept My Father's commandments and abide in His love.

I Corinthians 1:30

But by His doing you are in Christ Jesus, who became to us wisdom from God, and righteousness and sanctification, and redemption,

I Timothy 1:15-16

It is a trustworthy statement, deserving full acceptance, that Christ Jesus came into the world to save sinners, among whom I am foremost of all. Yet for this reason I found mercy, so that in me as the foremost, Jesus Christ might demonstrate His perfect patience as an example for those who would believe in Him for eternal life.

Matthew 9:12-13

But when Jesus heard this, He said, "It is not those who are healthy who need a physician, but those who are sick. "But go and learn what this means: 'I DESIRE COMPASSION, AND NOT SACRIFICE,' for I did not come to call the righteous, but sinners."

Mark 2:17

And hearing this, Jesus said to them, "It is not those who are healthy who need a physician, but those who are sick; I did not come to call the righteous, but sinners."

Luke 5:31-32

And Jesus answered and said to them, "It is not those who are well who need a physician, but those who are sick. "I have not come to call the righteous but sinners to repentance."

Hosea 6:6

For I delight in loyalty rather than sacrifice, And in the knowledge of God rather than burnt offerings.

Matthew 23:23

Woe to you, scribes and Pharisees, hypocrites! For you tithe mint and dill and cummin, and have neglected the weightier provisions of the law: justice and mercy and faithfulness; but these are the things you should have done without neglecting the others.

John 14:26

"But the Helper, the Holy Spirit, whom the Father will send in My name, He will teach you all things, and bring to your remembrance all that I said to you.

John 16:12-15

I have many more things to say to you, but you cannot bear them now. "But when He, the Spirit of truth, comes, He will guide you into all the truth; for He will not speak on His own initiative, but whatever He hears, He will speak; and He will disclose to you what is to come. "He will glorify Me, for He will take of Mine and will disclose it to you." All things that the Father has are Mine; therefore I said that He takes of Mine and will disclose it to you.

Romans 8:9

However, you are not in the flesh but in the Spirit, if indeed the Spirit of God dwells in you But if anyone does not have the Spirit of Christ, he does not belong to Him.

I Corinthians 2:11-13

For who among men knows the thoughts of a man except the spirit of the man which is in him? Even so the thoughts of God no one knows except the Spirit of God. Now we have received, not the spirit of the world, but the Spirit who is from God, so that we may know the things freely given to us by God, which things we also speak, not in words taught by human wisdom, but in those taught by the Spirit, combining spiritual thoughts with spiritual words.

Acts 16:6-7

They passed through the Phrygian and Galatian region, having been forbidden by the Holy Spirit to speak the word in Asia; and after they came to Mysia, they were trying to go into Bithynia, and the Spirit of Jesus did not permit them;

Acts 8:29

Then the Spirit said to Philip, "Go up and join this chariot."

Acts 10:19

While Peter was reflecting on the vision, the Spirit said to him, "Behold, three men are looking for you.

Acts 11:12

The Spirit told me to go with them without misgivings These six brethren also went with me and we entered the man's house.

Acts 13:2

While they were ministering to the Lord and fasting, the Holy Spirit said, "Set apart for Me Barnabas and Saul for the work to which I have called them."

Acts 15:28

For it seemed good to the Holy Spirit and to us to lay upon you no greater burden than these essentials:

1 Corinthians 2:14-16

But a natural man does not accept the things of the Spirit of God, for they are foolishness to him; and he cannot understand them, because they are spiritually appraised. But he who is spiritual appraises all things, yet he himself is appraised by no one. For WHO HAS KNOWN THE MIND OF THE LORD, THAT HE WILL INSTRUCT HIM? But we have the mind of Christ.

Philippians 2:5-11

Have this attitude in yourselves which was also in Christ Jesus, who, although He existed in the form of God, did not regard equality with God a thing to be grasped, but emptied Himself, taking the form of a bond-servant, and being made in the likeness of men. Being found in appearance as a man, He humbled Himself by becoming obedient to the point of death, even death on a cross. For this reason also, God highly exalted Him, and bestowed on Him the name which is above every name, so that at the name of Jesus EVERY KNEE WILL BOW, of those who are in heaven and on earth and under the earth, and that every tongue will confess that Jesus Christ is Lord, to the glory of God the Father.

1 Peter 4:1-2

Therefore, since Christ has suffered in the flesh, arm yourselves also with the same purpose, because he who has suffered in the flesh has ceased from sin, so as to live the rest of the time in the flesh no longer for the lusts of men, but for the will of God.

Printed in the United States
By Bookmasters